The Cambridge Pre-GED Program in READING

1988 Edition

CAMBRIDGE Adult Education
Prentice Hall Regents, Englewood Cliffs, NJ 07632

The Cambridge Pre-GED Program in
READING

Library of Congress Cataloging-in-Publication Data

The Cambridge pre-GED program in reading.—1988 ed.
   p. cm.
  ISBN 0-13-114265-8
   1. General educational development tests—Study guides.
  2. Reading (Secondary education)—Problems, exercises, etc.
  3. English language—Textbooks for foreign speakers.
LB3060.33.G45C366 1988   88-15002
428.4′076—dc19   CIP

Editorial supervision: Tim Foote
Production supervision: Janet Johnston
Manufacturing buyer: Art Michalez

 © 1988, 1983 by Prentice Hall Regents
Published by Prentice-Hall, Inc.
A Division of Simon & Schuster
Englewood Cliffs, New Jersey 07632

Printed in the United States of America

10 9 8 7 6 5 4 3 2

ISBN: 0-13-114265-8

Prentice-Hall International (UK) Limited, *London*
Prentice-Hall of Australia Pty. Limited, *Sydney*
Prentice-Hall Canada Inc., *Toronto*
Prentice-Hall Hispanoamericana, S.A., *Mexico*
Prentice-Hall of India Private Limited, *New Delhi*
Prentice-Hall of Japan, Inc., *Tokyo*
Simon & Schuster Asia Pte. Ltd., *Singapore*
Editora Prentice-Hall do Brasil, Ltda., *Rio de Janeiro*

CONTENTS

INTRODUCTION

With this book you can begin to prepare for three of the five tests that make up the GED, the High School Equivalency Exam. Those three tests are, in a way, tests of your reading skills. The Social Studies Test of the GED has 64 items that test your ability to understand and to think critically about social studies materials. Questions on the Science Test (66 items) and the Interpreting Literature and the Arts Test (45 items) also test your reading skills.

These are some of the features in this book that will help you with your GED preparation:

- The multiple-choice questions that make up the introductory and concluding tests are based on social studies, science, and literature materials. As on the GED, some of the questions are based on illustrations. The introductory test, beginning on page 4, will help you find out which of your reading skills need improvement. You should take that test before you begin your study in this book. The concluding test, on page 204, which you should take after you finish your study, will show you how your skills have improved. Both tests have Answer Keys, as well as Performance Analysis Charts for recording your scores. The charts also let you know which units in this book you should study.

- The instruction and practice material in this book is organized into five sections. Each concentrates on skills you will use when you take the GED. They will help you develop your skills at prereading, comprehending, and analyzing materials. One section concentrates on applying your skills to illustrations.

- Throughout the instruction there are practice exercises called **Try It**. Many of the questions in those exercises are similar to GED questions. In Units 2 and 3 there are sections called **Close-ups**. They will help you expand your social studies, science, and literature vocabulary.

- The Answers and Explanations at the end of each unit will help you check your work and clear up any mistakes.

You can use the *Cambridge Pre-GED Exercise Book in Reading* for extra practice as you work through this textbook. The charts on the inside covers of this book show which pages in the exercise book are related to the units in this book.

When you have successfully completed this book, you will have developed the reading skills you need to continue your preparation for the GED. You will then be able to move on to the instruction in Cambridge's GED books.

1

HOW MUCH CAN YOU DO ALREADY?

Before you begin to work in this book, take the test that starts on the next page. The test will show you how sharp your reading skills already are. It will also show you which units in this book you should study.

There are 40 questions on the test. They are based on different social studies and science passages and illustrations and on literature passages. The passages, illustrations, and questions are similar to many you will find on the GED. Try to answer all the questions.

After you finish the test, check your answers by using the answer key on page 17. Then fill in the chart on page 18. It will direct you to the units in this book you should concentrate on.

Read each passage. Then choose the correct answers to the questions that follow the passage.

America is said to be a nation of immigrants. That's because every group of people in America has come from a different land. Even the Indians came to America from Asia 20,000 years ago. Waves of immigrants have come to America looking for land, jobs, and religious and political freedom.

When the Declaration of Independence was signed, most Americans were of British background. Between 1790 and 1820, about 250,000 British and Western European immigrants came yearly. By 1840, almost 1 million immigrants arrived each year.

In the 1840s, a new group of immigrants started to arrive. Crop failures forced the Irish to emigrate. In the 1870s, many Chinese came to work for the railroads. Later, most of them returned to China. From the 1880s through 1900, Italians, Greeks, Poles, Slaves, and Jews came into the country. Almost 9 million people came to the U.S. between 1901 and 1910. After 1920, immigration fell sharply.

The level of immigration fell because Americans set quotas. Americans feared the customs and ways of new immigrants. Americans tried to limit the number of new people who entered the country.

1. The main idea of the passage is that America is

   (1) a nation of immigrant groups
   (2) a free country
   (3) a country that has quotas on immigration
   (4) a country that is made up mostly of British people

2. Which of the following is NOT stated as a reason that immigrants have come to America?

   (1) Immigrants have come to America looking for jobs.
   (2) Immigrants have come to America looking for land.
   (3) Immigrants have come to America to learn new customs.
   (4) Immigrants have come to America looking for religious freedom.

3. From the passage, you can infer that quotas on immigration were set up in America because

   (1) America was becoming too crowded
   (2) Americans began to fear the customs and ways of the new immigrants
   (3) there were not enough economic opportunities for the new immigrants
   (4) immigrants started to become violent

Why does one place have a high average temperature while another place has a low average temperature? Many things affect the average temperature of a place. One of those things is altitude.

Altitude is the height of a place. The top of a mountain, for example, has a higher altitude than the base of the mountain. Scientists usually begin their measurement of altitude at sea level, or the level of the surface of the sea.

Places at high altitudes have low temperatures. The top of a mountain has a lower temperature than the base of the mountain. The diagram below shows the temperature of a mountain at different altitudes. The average temperature drops about 3.5 degrees Fahrenheit for every 1,000 feet. This drop in temperature due to altitude is called the "normal lapse rate."

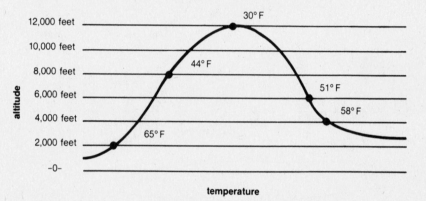

4. Which of the following statements best expresses the main idea of the passage?

   (1) The drop in temperature due to altitude is called the "normal lapse rate."
   (2) Altitude is one factor that affects the temperature of a place.
   (3) Altitude is the most important factor in the temperature of a place.
   (4) Scientists begin their measure of altitude at sea level.

5. For the mountain in the diagram, the air temperature at an altitude of 8,000 feet is

   (1) 65°F   (2) 58°F   (3) 51°F   (4) 44°F

6. Suppose you are at the base of a mountain. You climb to an altitude of 7,000 feet. Based on the information in the passage, you can conclude that at 7,000 feet the weather will be

   (1) drier   (2) warmer
   (3) cooler   (4) snowier

Average Hourly Concentrations of Two Types of Air Pollutants

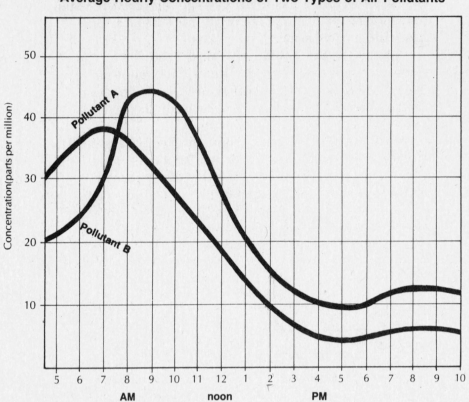

7. At which time of day are concentrations of Pollutant B at their highest?
   (1) 7:00 AM
   (2) 9:00 AM
   (3) 4:00 PM
   (4) 8:00 PM

8. What is the concentration of Pollutant A at 2 PM?

   (1) 20 parts per million
   (2) 15 parts per million
   (3) 10 parts per million
   (4) 2 parts per million

9. Based on the information in the graph, which of the following statements is true about the concentrations of both pollutants?

   (1) After 12:00 PM, they have the same concentrations.
   (2) They have higher concentrations in the morning than in the afternoon.
   (3) They both have concentration levels that reach higher than 40 parts per million.
   (4) They both have their highest concentration at 9:00 AM.

If someone tells you he fought in the Swiss Navy and speaks Swiss, don't believe a word he says. Switzerland is a landlocked nation. It hasn't gone to war in over a century. And there's no such thing as the Swiss language.

Switzerland is located among the highest mountains of western Europe. The Aar River flows in the north and the Rhone River cuts through the south. Many beautiful lakes serve as tourist attractions.

More than 6,300,000 people live in Switzerland. The national languages are German, French, and Italian. About 70% of the people speak German. Nearly everyone speaks at least two of the national languages. About 49% of the country is Roman Catholic, and 48% is Protestant.

Zurich is the largest city, with over 375,000 people. The capital, Bern, has a population of about 145,000. The city of Geneva is famous. The Red Cross was founded there, and the League of Nations started in Geneva after World War I.

The Swiss have a 99% literacy rate. This means that 99% of the people can read and write. Many children from other nations enroll in Swiss schools. The Swiss have a high standard of living. Foreign residents, who represent 20% of all workers, are willing to take the lower-paying jobs that the Swiss do not apply for.

The nation is a federation of 23 cantons. These states have a history of independence. Since 1848 they have joined to form a common government. But they still maintain their independent character.

10. Which of the following would make the best title for this passage?

   (1) Life in the Swiss Navy
   (2) The Cities of Switzerland
   (3) Facts About Switzerland
   (4) Languages of Switzerland

11. From the information in the passage, which of the following can be inferred about education in Switzerland?

   (1) There are more foreign students than Swiss students in Swiss schools.
   (2) The Swiss have a successful education system.
   (3) Most Swiss students go to schools in other countries.
   (4) Education is not important to the people of Switzerland.

12. The word *canton* in the last paragraph most nearly means

   (1) state   (3) federation
   (2) country   (4) city

Ernesto Miranda was arrested. Police charged him with assaulting and kidnapping a woman. He was placed in a police lineup, and the woman picked him out. Miranda confessed. After his confession had been used in court as evidence against him, Miranda was convicted. Simple enough?

Miranda's lawyer thought that if Miranda had known about the Fifth Amendment when he was arrested, the case might have turned out very differently. Part of the Fifth Amendment to the Constitution states that a suspect cannot be forced to be a witness against himself. Miranda's lawyer took the case to the Supreme Court.

Four of the judges felt that demanding police to read suspects their rights would overly complicate the job of law enforcement. But the other five judges ruled that the police had denied Miranda his rights under the Fifth Amendment. The lower court ruling was overturned, and Miranda was set free.

13. The passage implies that, when Ernesto Miranda was arrested, the police did not

    (1) let him call his lawyer
    (2) have any evidence against him
    (3) think he was guilty
    (4) tell him his rights

14. Which of the following statements from the passage is an OPINION?

    (1) Miranda was convicted of assaulting and kidnapping a woman.
    (2) If Miranda had known about his rights, his case would have turned out differently.
    (3) Miranda was set free because the Supreme Court ruled in his favor.
    (4) Part of the Fifth Amendment to the Constitution states that a suspect cannot be forced to be a witness against himself.

15. The passage implies that Miranda's lawyer took the case to the Supreme Court because

    (1) Miranda's rights had been violated
    (2) Miranda was innocent of the crime
    (3) Miranda did not really confess to the crime
    (4) there were no witnesses against Miranda

Ross Moschito's Paycheck

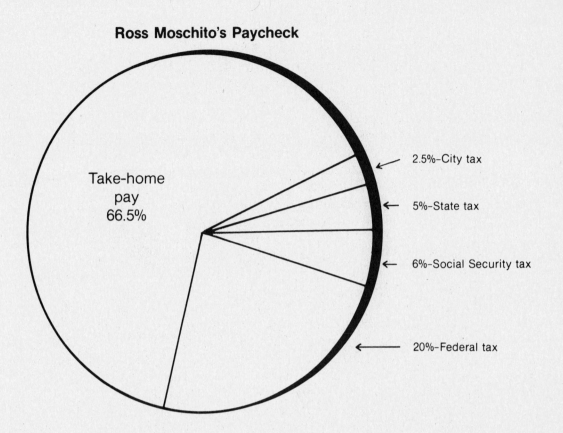

16. How much of Ross Moschito's paycheck goes to pay his federal tax?

    (1) 2.5%   (2) 5%   (3) 6%   (4) 20%

17. Which tax takes the least amount of money out of Ross Moschito's paycheck?

    (1) city tax
    (2) state tax
    (3) Social Security tax
    (4) federal tax

18. Which of the following statements about Ross Moschito's paycheck is supported by the graph?

    (1) Together, city, state, Social Security, and federal taxes take up most of Ross Moschito's paycheck.
    (2) More of Ross Moschito's money goes to pay for state tax than for Social Security tax.
    (3) Together, city, state, Social Security, and federal taxes take up about one third of Ross Moschito's paycheck.
    (4) Ross Moschito spends more money on taxes than he spends on rent and food.

Do you make more money than your parents do? Will your children live better than you do now? These are questions sociologists ask when they talk about social mobility. Social mobility is the movement from one class, or level of living, to another.

Most Americans are very concerned with upward mobility. Upward mobility is the improvement in a person's income, schooling, and class. Most Americans try to live better than their parents did.

Sociologists ask whether American institutions encourage upward mobility. They ask whether America has an open-class system or a closed-class system. In an open-class system, many people improve their living standards. In a closed-class system, most people live at the same level as their parents did.

Some sociologists think that America has an open-class system. They point to unions that keep the wages and living standards of laborers high. They point to open-door colleges that give children of poor parents a good education. Other sociologists think that America has a closed-class system. They say that only the wealthy can afford the very good schools. They add that racial and economic prejudice keeps minorities from moving into better job positions.

19. Which of the following would make the best title for the passage?

    (1) Sociologists
    (2) America—An Open-Class System
    (3) A Look at Social Mobility
    (4) Racial and Economic Prejudice in America

20. Which of the following would NOT be an example of how an open-class system works?

    (1) A student from a poor family gets a free college education.
    (2) A labor union gets a big pay increase for its workers.
    (3) A young woman can't get a good job because she doesn't have the money to stay in school.
    (4) 85% of the people in a country have an improvement in their standard of living.

21. According to the passage, sociologists use the term "social mobility" to mean

    (1) the movement from one class, or level of living, to another
    (2) the improvement in a person's income, schooling, and class
    (3) the existence of an open-class system in a society
    (4) the existence of a closed-class system in a society

I hadn't been open more than ten minutes when Doc Stair come in. He looked kind of nervous. He asked me had I seen Paul Dickson. I said no, but I knew where he was, out duck-shootin' with Jim Kendall. So Doc says that's what he had heard, and he couldn't understand it because Paul had told him he wouldn't never have no more to do with Jim as long as he lived.

He said Paul had told him about the joke Jim had played on Julie. He said Paul had asked him what he thought of the joke and the Doc had told him that anybody that would do a thing like that ought not be let live.

I said it had been a kind of a raw thing, but Jim just couldn't resist no kind of a joke, no matter how raw. I said I thought he was all right at heart, but just bubblin' over with mischief. Doc turned and walked out.

At noon he got a phone call from old John Scott. The lake where Jim and Paul had went shootin' is on John's place. Paul had came runnin' up to the house a few minutes before and said they'd been an accident. Jim had shot a few ducks and then give the gun to Paul and told him to try his luck. Paul hadn't never handled a gun and he was nervous. He was shakin' so hard that he couldn't control the gun. He let fire and Jim sunk back in the boat, dead.

22. Based on the information in the passage, Doc Stair thinks it is odd that Paul went with Jim because Paul

   (1) didn't like jokes
   (2) didn't like duck hunting
   (3) didn't know how to handle a gun
   (4) didn't want anything to do with Jim

23. Based on the information in the passage, you can infer that Jim's death might have been

   (1) a practical joke
   (2) a suicide
   (3) a murder
   (4) a boating accident

24. The author's writing style is like the style of a

   (1) speech
   (2) conversation
   (3) poem
   (4) joke

The work of French scientist Jean Baptiste Lamarck (1744–1829) has contributed to the theory of evolution.

Lamarck believed that the environment shaped the development of plant and animal life. He believed that the bodies of plants and animals changed to fit their environment. He thought that a useful physical change would be passed on to the plant's or animal's offspring.

For example, Lamarck thought that giraffes developed long necks because they had to stretch to reach the leaves of tall trees for food. Lamarck didn't think that giraffes developed long necks all at once, however. He thought that the earliest group of giraffes stretched their necks a small amount. Their offspring inherited this longer neck. The offspring then stretched their necks a little bit more. They passed this even longer neck on to their own offspring. Over many generations, giraffes developed the long necks that they have today.

Not all of Lamarck's theory is accepted today. Most scientists do believe that the environment has an effect on the evolution of life forms. But they don't agree with the theory that a physical change in a plant's or animal's body is passed on to the offspring. Instead, they believe that a change must occur in the plant's or animal's cells before a change in the offspring can take place.

25. The main purpose of the passage is to discuss

   (1) the theory of evolution
   (2) the work of Jean Baptiste Lamarck
   (3) the evolution of giraffes
   (4) beliefs held by today's scientists

26. According to the passage, Lamarck believed that the development of plant and animal life was shaped by the plant's or animal's

   (1) cells   (3) environment
   (2) offspring   (4) physical traits

27. Based on the information in the passage, with which of the following statements about Lamarck's work would most scientists today agree?

   (1) None of Lamarck's theory about evolution makes sense.
   (2) An animal that changes physically will always pass on the change to its offspring.
   (3) Giraffes are the only animals that have changed through evolution.
   (4) Environment can cause a change in the bodies of plants and animals.

You always hated to say anything against the owners because you were made to feel you were lucky to be playing baseball. You should be thankful for it. Never mind you're not getting a fair shake, you're lucky to be there and you shouldn't ever, but never, criticize the major league owners or the administration. One of the first things my coach in college told me when I went into pro baseball: "Don't be a clubhouse lawyer."

"The good of the game" is what you hear so much about. Everything owners do is for "the good of the game." They talk about baseball as a sport. But they move teams around from city to city strictly for money. A new team in Seattle two years ago cost the people about five million dollars. It sold for a tremendous amount. Here's a club that's supposed to be losing a lot of money. Yet there was an interested buyer. No club in baseball loses money. Every club makes money. I don't see how you could call it a sport. It's big business.

A lot of owners don't really want to know players. Then you become more than a name. You become more than a piece of paper they can trade or sell or release. They insist on knowing you as a thing. It's easy for them to manipulate. But when you become involved with somebody, it's difficult. The only way to run a successful baseball operation is to treat the players as things.

28. According to the passage, the term "clubhouse lawyer" most likely refers to someone who

   (1) is lucky to be playing baseball
   (2) hates to say anything against the owners
   (3) criticizes the administration
   (4) moves teams from city to city

29. Which of the following best describes the author's attitude toward the baseball owners?

   (1) angry
   (2) unconcerned
   (3) proud
   (4) understanding

30. Which of the following statements can be concluded from the passage?

   (1) Most baseball owners know the players well.
   (2) Few baseball owners make money from their teams.
   (3) Baseball owners often do not ask players if they want to be traded.
   (4) Owners move teams to new cities for "the good of the game."

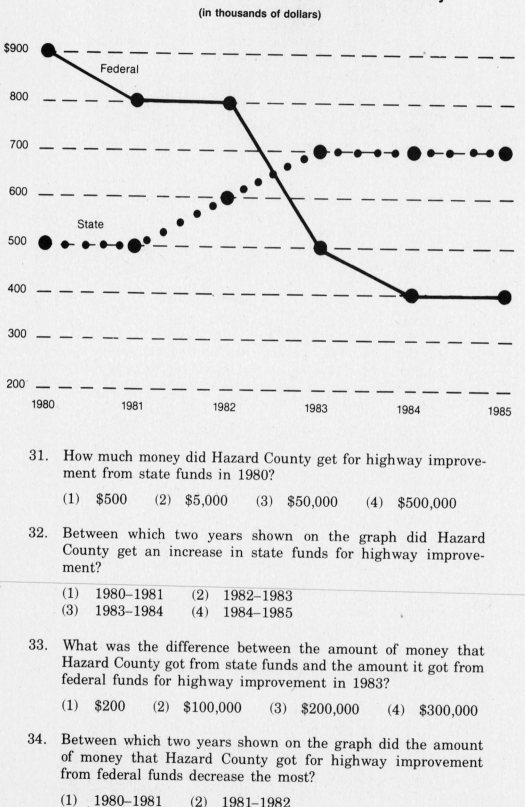

Funding for Highway Improvement in Hazard County

(in thousands of dollars)

31. How much money did Hazard County get for highway improvement from state funds in 1980?

    (1) $500   (2) $5,000   (3) $50,000   (4) $500,000

32. Between which two years shown on the graph did Hazard County get an increase in state funds for highway improvement?

    (1) 1980–1981   (2) 1982–1983
    (3) 1983–1984   (4) 1984–1985

33. What was the difference between the amount of money that Hazard County got from state funds and the amount it got from federal funds for highway improvement in 1983?

    (1) $200   (2) $100,000   (3) $200,000   (4) $300,000

34. Between which two years shown on the graph did the amount of money that Hazard County got for highway improvement from federal funds decrease the most?

    (1) 1980–1981   (2) 1981–1982
    (3) 1982–1983   (4) 1983–1984

Dieters aren't the only people who talk about calories. Scientists measure heat in units known as calories.

Heat is the energy that flows between a thing and its surroundings. If a thing has a higher temperature than its surroundings, energy flows away from the thing. If a thing has a lower temperature than its surroundings, energy flows to the thing. This energy, while it is in transit, is called heat.

Scientists measure weight in units known as grams. They measure temperature in Celsius degrees. And heat is measured in units known as calories.

What exactly is a calorie? It can't be marked on a ruler or a scale. A calorie is the amount of heat needed to raise the temperature of 1 gram of water by 1 degree Celsius. Suppose that you have a test tube that contains one gram of water. When you put a flame under the test tube, energy is transferred from the flame to the test tube in the form of heat. Suppose that the temperature of the water rises 4 degrees Celsius. Four calories of heat energy are used.

When people say that food has calories, they are really talking about the amount of energy that could be released when the food is used by the body. Calories by themselves don't necessarily make you gain weight. It's only when calories are stored, and not used, that weight can be gained.

35. The main purpose of this passage is to discuss

    (1) heat   (3) energy
    (2) water   (4) calories

36. In the passage, a "calorie" is defined as

    (1) the amount of heat needed to raise the temperature of 1 gram of water by 1 degree Celsius
    (2) the transference of heat from a thing to its surroundings
    (3) the amount of fats and sugars that are contained in one gram of food
    (4) the amount of stored energy that is needed to raise the weight of a person by 1 gram

37. Which of the following statements about calories can be inferred from the passage?

    (1) A calorie does not have size or weight.
    (2) Calories are not important to people who are on diets.
    (3) Calories can only be stored by the human body.
    (4) Calories can be added to water simply by heating the water.

It's a funny thing that all of us get up every morning and set out to make progress. When you think about some of the things that progress has brought us, it isn't all that good sometimes.

It is sad for me to report to you that progress has set in at our vegetable stand. We always waited with great excitement for those great, red-ripe, thin-skinned tomatoes. Last week we stopped at the stand, and they had tomatoes all right, but not the tomatoes that took me four miles off course to buy. These were the pink, perfectly formed, tough, tasteless kind. They give the idea that they weren't so much grown as manufactured. The only thing they're good for is as decoration on a salad plate. You can't really eat them. They're to be used like parsley in a restaurant that serves small portions but wants to fill the blank spaces on the plate.

The beauty of these square tomatoes is that they can be picked by machine and shipped for thousands of miles over a period of months without rotting. I suspect it wouldn't hurt one of them much if one of the trucks behind the picking machines ran over it. The driver might think he'd hit a rock, but no real damage would be done to either the truck or the tomato.

If I am ever elected to Congress, I think I'll try to get a law passed making tomatoes illegal, except for certain months of the year. I have spent more money on hard, tasteless tomatoes in the last ten years than I've spent on toothpaste, shoelaces and typewriter ribbons combined. I never learn. I look at them and my memory of how good they used to be in season makes me reach for my money.

The U.S. government has sponsored research that has produced a tomato that is perfect in every way, except you can't eat it. We should make every effort to make sure this disease, often referred to as "progress," doesn't spread.

38. Which of the following statements from the passage is a fact and not an opinion?

(1) Last week we stopped at the stand, and they had tomatoes all right . . .
(2) They give the idea that they weren't so much grown as manufactured.
(3) The only thing they're good for is as decoration on a salad plate.
(4) We should make every effort to make sure this disease, often referred to as "progress," doesn't spread.

39. At one point in the passage, the author compares the tomatoes to

    (1) trucks   (3) tires
    (2) rocks   (4) machines

40. Which of the following statements expresses the author's main point?

    (1) Tomatoes today are good only as decorations on salad plates.
    (2) The machines that pick tomatoes still need to be improved.
    (3) Tomatoes should be made illegal, except for certain months of the year.
    (4) Growing and picking tomatoes through mass production is not progress.

ANSWER KEY

1. (1)	11. (2)	21. (1)	31. (4)
2. (3)	12. (1)	22. (4)	32. (2)
3. (2)	13. (4)	23. (3)	33. (3)
4. (2)	14. (2)	24. (2)	34. (3)
5. (4)	15. (1)	25. (2)	35. (4)
6. (3)	16. (4)	26. (3)	36. (1)
7. (2)	17. (1)	27. (4)	37. (1)
8. (3)	18. (3)	28. (3)	38. (1)
9. (2)	19. (3)	29. (1)	39. (2)
10. (3)	20. (3)	30. (3)	40. (4)

In this chart, circle the number of any item that you did not answer correctly. The right-hand side of the chart will tell you the units to study for any item that you missed.

Item number:	Unit to study:
12 28	UNIT 3: Using Clues to Unlock Word Meanings
1 4 25	UNIT 4: Finding the Main Idea
2 21 22 26 36 39	UNIT 5: Finding Details
10 19 35 40	UNIT 6: Finding the Unstated Main Idea
3 11 13 15 20 23 37	UNIT 7: Making Basic Inferences; UNIT 8: Using Organization to Make Inferences
6 18 30	UNIT 9: Drawing Logical Conclusions
14 24 27 29 38	UNIT 10: Recognizing Facts and Opinions; UNIT 11: Identifying Bias and Tone
5 7 8 9 16 17 31 32 33 34	UNIT 12: Reading Tables, Graphs, Diagrams, and Maps

Before you do any other work in this book, study the section "Taking the First Step," which begins on the next page.

Taking the First Step

You probably read a lot of different things every day. You may read directions on a label. You may read a menu in a diner. You may read stories in the newspaper. You may read fictional stories for pleasure.

The things that you read can be very different from one another. The directions on a medicine bottle are a lot different from a newspaper story. But there are things that you can do to make *all* kinds of reading a little easier.

In the following section of this book, you'll look at some reading strategies. These strategies are ideas that you can use to make reading a little easier. You probably already use most of these strategies on the kinds of things you read every day. This section will show you how you can also use these strategies on the kinds of written passages you will find on the three "reading" tests on the GED.

UNIT 1: PREVIEWING, SCANNING, AND PREDICTING

PREVIEWING

What's the first thing you do when you read a newspaper story? Chances are, the first thing you do is look at the story's headline. A headline often tells you a lot about a story. For example, look at this headline:

THREE MEN HURT
IN CAR ACCIDENT

Can you tell what the story is about? The story is about a car accident. Three men were hurt in the accident. The headline gives you this information. You get all this information before you even start to read the story.

The first thing to do when you read something is to find out a little bit about it. Newspaper headlines tell you about the stories in a newspaper. Newspaper headlines give you a **preview** of the stories. A preview is a look at something in advance.

Previewing is an important part of reading. It's important because it helps you to prepare yourself for what you are reading. It helps you to think about the information you are reading.

It's pretty easy to preview a newspaper story. All you have to do is read the headline. But some things that you read don't have headlines. You have to find other ways to preview them. Look at this reading passage:

Sleeping pills are a popular drug in America. But some people—including many doctors—think they are too popular.

Every day, about 30 million sleeping pills are taken in America. This means that, in a year, Americans take 600 tons of sleeping pills. That's enough to put everyone in the country to sleep for eight days.

Sleeping pills are sedatives. They relax the body and help it to sleep. But sleeping pills can have dangerous side effects. A person who uses sleeping pills too often can become addicted to them. Also, a person who takes too many sleeping pills at once can suffer from a drug overdose. An overdose of sleeping pills can cause death.

This passage doesn't have a headline. It doesn't have any title on it. How can you preview this passage? What can you do to find out something about it before you read it?

The first thing that you can do is simple. Read the first sentence of the passage:

Sleeping pills are a popular drug in America. But some people—including many doctors—think they are too popular.

Does the first sentence give you an idea of what the passage is about? The first sentence is about sleeping pills. The first sentence gives you the idea that the passage is about sleeping pills.

But can you be sure of this? Maybe the first sentence doesn't tell you about the rest of the passage. Is there a quick way to check the information in the first sentence?

There *is* a quick way to check the information. It's called **scanning**.

SCANNING

Think about this. Suppose you are thirsty. You want to buy something to drink. You walk into a fast-food place. You don't want to buy anything to eat. You just want to buy something to drink.

You go up to the cash register. Behind the cash register, there is a menu. It tells you everything that the fast-food place has to sell. You take a look at the menu to see what you can buy to drink.

BurgerQuick

menu

BURGERS		FRIES	
Plain burger	$1.00	Small fries	$ .85
Cheeseburger	$1.25	Big fries	$1.10
BQ Special	$1.85	Super fries	$1.50

SANDWICHES		DRINKS	
Fish	$2.00	Small soda	$ .75
Roast Beef	$2.75	Big soda	$1.00
Chicken	$2.75	Big shake	$1.25
		Coffee/tea	$ .60

Did you read the whole menu? Did you read every single thing on the menu? Or did you do something else?

Chances are, you didn't read everything. Chances are, you only read part of the menu. You only read the part of the menu labeled "DRINKS." You *scanned* the menu to find what you were looking for.

When you scanned the menu, you took a quick look at it. You didn't try to read everything on the menu. Instead, you looked quickly for the information you needed. Then you read only that information.

Scanning is a very short process. It only takes a few seconds. But scanning can be very helpful. It can help you to find information quickly. It can help you to get some ideas about a reading passage.

Think back to the passage on the last page. You read the first sentence of the passage. The first sentence is about sleeping pills. How would you scan the passage to check what it is about? Can you tell quickly if the rest of the passage is about sleeping pills?

Sleeping pills are a popular drug in America. But some people—including many doctors—think they are too popular.

Every day, about 30 million **sleeping pills** are taken in America. This means that, in a year, Americans take 600 tons of **sleeping pills**. That's enough to put everyone in the country to sleep for eight days.

Sleeping pills are sedatives. They relax the body and help it to sleep. But **sleeping pills** can have dangerous side effects. A person who uses **sleeping pills** too often can become addicted to them. Also, a person who takes too many **sleeping pills** at once can suffer from a drug overdose. An overdose of **sleeping pills** can cause death.

When you scan, you can see that sleeping pills are mentioned often in the passage. The first sentence tells about sleeping pills. Together, these two things give you a good preview of the passage. You have a good idea that the passage is about sleeping pills.

Previewing is an important part of reading. It helps you to find out a little about the thing that you are reading. It helps you to think about the information you are reading.

Scanning is a process that you can use in previewing. When you scan something, you take a quick look at it. You don't read every word. Scanning can help you to find information quickly. It can help you to get some ideas about a reading passage.

Try It: Using Previewing and Scanning

Preview the next two reading passages. First, underline the first sentence. See if the sentence gives you an idea of what the passage is about. Then, scan the passage. Look for key words that tell you what the passage is about. Underline the key words. After you have previewed each passage, answer the question that follows it.

People spend a lot of time watching TV. But how much TV does the average person watch? A survey shows that the average person watches nearly 30 hours of TV every week. Men who are over age 55 watch TV the most. They spend about 38½ hours a week in front of a TV set. Teenage girls watch TV the least. They only spend about 22 hours a week watching TV.

The most popular time to watch TV is in the evening. The average person spends more than 9 hours a week watching TV between 8 PM and 11 PM. This is why evening TV shows are called "prime-time" shows.

1. What is this passage about?

Income taxes are a big part of American life. Without income taxes, the government would run out of money. But income taxes weren't always so important. In fact, there was a time when income taxes were *illegal*.

In 1894, the U.S. Congress passed an income-tax law. But the Supreme Court ruled that the law could not be used. The Court said that the Constitution did not allow the U.S. government to collect income taxes. The new income-tax law could not be used because it went against the Constitution.

However, things changed. In 1913, the Constitution was changed. It was changed to allow the U.S. government to collect income taxes. It wasn't long before a new income-tax law was passed.

2. What is this passage about?

Check your answers on page 30.

PREDICTING

Previewing is an important first step in reading. When you preview, you get an idea of what a passage is about. You get an idea by finding the passage's **topic**.

What is a topic? A topic is the subject of a passage. It is the main thing that the passage is about.

You previewed this passage in the last exercise:

People spend a lot of time watching TV. But how much TV does the average person watch? A survey shows that the average person watches nearly 30 hours of TV every week. Men who are over age 55 watch TV the most. They spend about 38½ hours a week in front of a TV set. Teenage girls watch TV the least. They only spend about 22 hours a week watching TV.

The most popular time to watch TV is in the evening. The average person spends more than 9 hours a week watching TV between 8 PM and 11 PM. This is why evening TV shows are called "prime-time" shows.

What is this passage about? By previewing, you can get a good idea that the passage is about watching TV. *Watching TV* is the topic of the passage. It is the subject of the passage. You have a good idea that the passage will tell you something about watching TV.

But what will the passage tell you about watching TV? Previewing won't give you the answer to this. Remember, previewing only takes a few seconds. You only get a quick idea about the passage when you preview. You only get an idea of the topic. You have to do more to find out what the passage says about the topic. You have to begin to read the passage.

Some passages are harder to read than others. But there is a step that can make all passages a little easier to read. That step is called **predicting**.

What do you do when you predict something? You try to figure out what is going to happen. You make a guess about what is going to happen.

How do you predict something? You predict by using information that you know. For example, think about this. Suppose you walk outside one morning. You look up at the sky. You don't see the sun shining. Instead, you see a lot of dark clouds. You hear some thunder in the distance.

What do you think is going to happen?

You might predict that it's going to rain. You see the dark clouds. You hear the thunder. You know that dark clouds and thunder usually mean rain. Using this information, you make a prediction. You predict that it will probably rain.

Predicting is helpful in everyday life. It helps you to expect things. If you expect something to happen, you won't be surprised by it. For example, suppose you predict that it will probably rain. You expect it to rain. If you are going for a long walk, you may decide to take an umbrella with you. You won't be surprised if it rains. You'll be ready for it.

You can also use predicting when you read. Predicting can help you to get ready for the information in a passage. This way, you won't be surprised by the passage. You'll find the information in the passage a little easier to read.

How can you use predicting when you read? Follow these steps:

1. Preview the passage to get an idea of what the topic is.
2. Go back to the beginning of the story. Read the first three sentences of the story.
3. Stop. Think about what you have read. Do you have an idea of what the passage will probably tell you about the topic?

Here is a passage that you've never seen before. Take a few seconds to preview it, but don't read it all. After you preview, go to the question that follows the passage.

Otto von Kleinschmidt is a German prince. Prince Otto has a hobby. His hobby is painting with jet engines.

How can Prince Otto paint with a jet engine? You almost have to see it to believe it. First, Prince Otto sets up a large canvas. He puts the canvas right behind the engine of a jet. The engine is started up. Prince Otto then takes a bucket of paint. He flings the paint toward the engine. The air from the engine blows against the paint. It pushes the paint back toward the canvas. The paint splatters against the canvas. Prince Otto has created another painting.

If you think that Prince Otto sounds silly, think about this. He has sold five of his jet-engine paintings. He sold the paintings for $100,000 *each*. That's a half million dollars altogether. Prince Otto von Kleinschmidt doesn't seem so silly after all.

From previewing, did you get an idea of what the topic of the passage is? You read about Otto von Kleinschmidt in the first sentence. As you scanned the passage, you probably saw Prince Otto's name appear several times. From previewing, you probably got the idea that the passage is about Prince Otto.

What does the passage say about Prince Otto? Before you answer this question, read the first three sentences of the passage:

Otto von Kleinschmidt is a German prince. Prince
Otto has a hobby. His hobby is painting with jet engines.

Can you predict what the rest of the passage will say about Prince Otto?

The first sentence tells you who Otto von Kleinschmidt is. The second sentence tells you that Prince Otto has a hobby. The third sentence tells you what his hobby is. It sounds like a pretty strange hobby. You could predict that the rest of the passage will be about Prince Otto's hobby.

Now, read the rest of the passage. See if your prediction was right.

How can Prince Otto paint with a jet engine? You
almost have to see it to believe it. First, Prince Otto sets
up a large canvas. He puts the canvas right behind the
engine of a jet. The engine is started up. Prince Otto
then takes a bucket of paint. He flings the paint toward
the engine. The air from the engine blows against the
paint. It pushes the paint back toward the canvas. The
paint splatters against the canvas. Prince Otto has
created another painting.

If you think that Prince Otto sounds silly, think
about this. He has sold five of his jet-engine paintings.
He sold the paintings for $100,000 *each*. That's a half
million dollars altogether. Prince Otto von Kleinschmidt
doesn't seem so silly after all.

The rest of the passage *does* tell you about Prince Otto's hobby. First, it describes the hobby. Then it tells you that Prince Otto has made a lot of money from his hobby. Your prediction about the passage was right.

Most of the time, your predictions will be right. But it's not always easy to predict what a passage will tell you. For example, look at the beginning of this passage:

Armand Peters is a successful lawyer. Last year, his
income was greater than $100,000. But, two months ago,
Armand Peters filed for bankruptcy.

Can you predict what this passage will be about? The first three sentences are about Armand Peters. The first sentence tells you who Armand Peters is. The second sentence tells you that Armand Peters made a lot of money last year. The third sentence tells you that Armand Peters has filed for bankruptcy. Armand Peters has run out of money even though he made more than $100,000 last year. You could predict that the rest of the passage will tell you how and why Armand Peters has run out of money.

Now, read the rest of the passage to check your prediction:

Lucille Nevers owns three restaurants in Dallas, Texas. The three restaurants give Lucille Nevers a profit that averages $2,500 per week. Last month, Lucille Nevers filed for bankruptcy.

Armand Peters and Lucille Nevers are just two of the many Americans who will go to court this year to file for protection under the U.S. bankruptcy laws.

What does it mean to file for bankruptcy? A person who files for bankruptcy claims that he does not have enough money or property to pay his bills. If the court finds that the person really can't pay his debts, the court declares that the person is bankrupt. All the money that the person has gets divided among the people to whom he owes money. But any bills that aren't paid get torn up once all the money is gone. The person gets to start all over.

The rest of the passage does *not* tell you how and why Armand Peters has run out of money. First, it tells you about Lucille Nevers. Then it tells you something about bankruptcy. The passage tells you what it means to file for bankruptcy.

Sometimes, it's hard to predict what a passage will be about. You won't be able to predict what every passage will be about. But it's still a good idea to use predicting when you read. Predicting can help you to get ready for the information in a passage. It can help to make the information in the passage a little easier to read.

Try It: Predicting

Here is a reading passage. Before you read the passage, preview it. After you preview the passage, answer the question that follows it.

The amount of money that businesses spend on advertising is almost unbelievable. Experts say that, in a year, businesses spend more than $60 billion on advertising in the United States alone.

Which kinds of businesses spend the most on advertising? Experts say that the food industry is one of the biggest advertisers. Eleven of the top fifty advertisers in the United States are food companies. Companies that make cosmetics also advertise a lot. Five of the top fifty advertisers are cosmetics companies. Other kinds of businesses that spend a lot of money on advertising are automobile makers, drug companies, retail stores, and cigarette makers.

1. What is the topic of this passage?

Here are the first three sentences of the passage. Read them. Then stop and try to answer the question that follows them.

The amount of money that businesses spend on advertising is almost unbelievable. Experts say that, in a year, businesses spend more than $60 billion on advertising in the United States alone.

Which kinds of businesses spend the most on advertising?

2. What do you predict this passage will be about?

Now, read the rest of the passage. See if your prediction was right.

3. What is the passage about? Was your prediction right?

Here is another passage. Before you read it, preview it. After you preview it, answer the question that follows it.

If you have a kitchen table, chances are that you have a salt shaker on it. Salt is a very popular food seasoning. But many doctors warn that salt may be *too* popular. Tests show that salt is linked to high blood pressure in humans. People who eat too much salt have a greater chance of having high blood pressure than people who don't eat much salt. High blood pressure is a disease that can be deadly.

Many doctors feel that there is one good way to control the amount of salt you eat. That way is to put away your salt shaker. Many foods already have salt in them. You don't really need to add salt to them. But if you can't do without salt, there's another thing you can do. Try tasting your food *before* you add salt to it. Doctors say that too many people put salt on their food before they eat. They don't taste the food first to see if it even needs salt.

4. What is the topic of this passage?

Here are the first three sentences of the passage. Read them. Then stop and try to answer the question that follows them.

If you have a kitchen table, chances are that you have a salt shaker on it. Salt is a very popular food seasoning. But many doctors warn that salt may be *too* popular.

5. What do you predict this passage will be about?

Now, read the rest of the passage. See if your prediction was right.

6. What is the passage about? Was your prediction right?

Check your answers on page 31.

UNIT REVIEW

In this unit, you've taken a look at three basic reading processes: **previewing**, **scanning**, and **predicting**. A preview is a look at something in advance. When you preview a reading passage, you get an idea about it before you read it. Scanning is a part of previewing. When you scan something, you take a quick look at it. When you scan a reading passage, you don't read every word. Instead, you look for key words that may tell you what the passage is about.

The third process that you looked at is predicting. When you predict, you make a guess. The guess is based on information that you know. You can use information that you get from previewing to predict what a passage is about. You can also use information in the beginning of the passage to make a prediction.

Previewing, scanning, and predicting can all make reading a little easier. They can help you to prepare for the information that a reading passage contains. They can help you to know what to expect when you read a passage. In the next unit, you'll look at another process that can make reading a little easier. You'll look at how information is put together in a reading passage.

ANSWERS AND EXPLANATIONS

Try It: Using Previewing and Scanning

1. This passage is about **watching TV**. The first sentence tells you that people spend a lot of time watching TV. As you scanned the passage, you probably saw the words "watch TV" or "watching TV" several times:

> People spend a lot of time watching TV. But how much TV does the average person watch? A survey shows that the average person watches nearly 30 hours of TV every week. Men who are over age 55 watch TV the most. They spend about 38½ hours a week in front of a TV set. Teenage girls watch TV the least. They only spend about 22 hours a week watching TV.
>
> The most popular time to watch TV is in the evening. The average person spends more than 9 hours a week watching TV between 8 PM and 11 PM. This is why evening TV shows are called "prime-time" shows.

2. This passage is about **income taxes**. The first sentence tells you that income taxes are a big part of American life. As you scanned the passage, you probably saw the words "income taxes" several times:

> Income taxes are a big part of American life. Without income taxes, the government would run out of money. But income taxes weren't always so important. In fact, there was a time when income taxes were *illegal*.
>
> In 1894, the U.S. Congress passed an income-tax law. But the Supreme Court ruled that the law could not be used. The Court said that the Constitution did not allow the U.S. government to collect income taxes. The new income-tax law could not be used because it went against the Constitution.
>
> However, things changed. In 1913, the Constitution was changed. It was changed to allow the U.S. government to collect income taxes. It wasn't long before a new income-tax law was passed.

Try It: Predicting

1. From previewing, you could guess that the topic of the passage is **advertising**. The first sentence of the passage tells you about the amount of money that businesses spend on advertising. As you scanned the passage, you probably saw the words "advertising," "advertisers," and "advertise" several times.

2. You could have predicted that the passage will be about the **businesses that spend the most money on advertising**. The first two sentences tell you about the amount of money that businesses spend on advertising. The third sentence asks a question: "Which kinds of businesses spend the most on advertising?" You could predict that the rest of the passage will answer this question.

3. The passage gives you information about the kinds of businesses that spend the most money on advertising. It lists some of the industries that spend the most money. If you predicted this, you were right.

4. From previewing, you could guess that the topic of the passage is **salt**. The first sentence mentions a salt shaker. As you scanned the passage, you probably saw the word *salt* several times.

5. You could have predicted that the passage will be about why doctors think that salt is too popular. The second sentence tells you that salt is a very popular food. The third sentence says that some doctors think that it is too popular. You could predict that the rest of the passage will explain why they think salt is too popular.

6. The passage is about the health problems that salt may cause. It also tells you things you can do to cut down on the amount of salt that you eat. The first three sentences didn't give you a clue about the second part of the passage. But they did give you enough information to predict that the passage would tell you about the health problems that salt may cause.

UNIT 2: KEEPING TRACK OF IDEAS AS YOU READ

In Unit 1, you looked at using previewing, scanning, and predicting when you read. Previewing and scanning can help you to get an idea about the topic of a passage. Predicting can help you to understand what the passage will say about the topic.

But a passage usually has a lot of information in it. You can't always remember everything that you read in a passage. Sometimes, you have to look back to find a piece of information. Sometimes, you have to look back to find the answer to a question.

Looking back to find a piece of information can be hard. But there's something you can do to make it easier. You can try to keep track of where things are in a passage as you read it. Keeping track of ideas will help to make the ideas a lot easier to find.

LOOKING AT ORGANIZATION

Suppose you walk into a BurgerQuick fast-food place. You want to get a sandwich. You want to get a *chicken* sandwich. You want to find out how much a chicken sandwich costs. You look up at the menu:

BurgerQuick

menu

BURGERS		**FRIES**	
Plain burger	$1.00	Small fries	$ .85
Cheeseburger	$1.25	Big fries	$1.10
BQ Special	$1.85	Super fries	$1.50
SANDWICHES		**DRINKS**	
Fish	$2.00	Small soda	$ .75
Roast Beef	$2.75	Big soda	$1.00
Chicken	$2.75	Big shake	$1.25
		Coffee/tea	$ .60

Did you have to read the whole menu? Or did you take a short cut to find out how much a chicken sandwich costs?

Chances are, you took a short cut. First, you probably looked for the heading "SANDWICHES." Then, you probably looked down the list of things under the heading. You looked until you came to the word "Chicken." When you came to "Chicken," you stopped. You looked across at the price. The price told you how much a chicken sandwich costs.

You probably used this short cut without even thinking about it. Why were you able to use it? You could use the short cut because you saw how the information on the menu is **organized**. You saw how the things on the menu are put together. It was easy to use the short cut once you knew how to find what you were looking for.

Everything that you read is made up of information and ideas. Everything is organized in a certain way. Reading is easier when you know how things are put together. It's easier because it helps you to find a piece of information when you look back for it. It helps you to keep track of things as you read.

Read the next passage. As you read, think about how the information in the passage is organized.

Most Americans now have a TV set in their home. TV sets are pretty trusty—they don't break too often. But when they *do* break, they have to be fixed. Usually, they have to be fixed by a TV repair shop.

Getting your TV fixed can cost a lot of money. But there are three things you can do to make sure that you're not paying *too* much money. First, check to see if the TV is covered by a warranty. If it is, chances are that you won't have to pay much to get the TV fixed. Second, ask the repair shop to tell you what is wrong with the TV *before* it gets fixed. Ask for an estimate of how much it will cost to have the TV fixed. (Be careful, though—sometimes you might have to pay for an estimate.) You may also want to compare estimates from several shops to see which one is the cheapest. Third, read the repair bill *before* you pay it. Make sure that you understand all the charges before you pay them. Don't be afraid to ask questions—they can save you money.

What is this passage about? The passage is about getting a TV set fixed. What does it tell you about getting a TV set fixed? It lists three things to do to make sure that you're not paying too much to get your TV fixed.

How is the information in the passage put together? The answer to this question is pretty easy. There are two basic parts to this passage. The first part gives you an introduction to the passage. It lets you know what the passage will be about. The second part tells you the three things to do when you get your TV fixed.

1. Introduction

Most Americans now have a TV set in their home. TV sets are pretty trusty—they don't break too often. But when they *do* break, they have to be fixed. Usually, they have to be fixed by a TV repair shop.

2. List of things to do when you get your TV fixed

Getting your TV fixed can cost a lot of money. But there are three things you can do to make sure that you're not paying *too* much money. First, check to see if the TV is covered by a warranty. If it is, chances are that you won't have to pay much to get the TV fixed. Second, ask the repair shop to tell you what is wrong with the TV *before* it gets fixed. Ask for an estimate of how much it will cost to have the TV fixed. (Be careful, though—sometimes you might have to pay for an estimate.) You may also want to compare estimates from several shops to see which one is the cheapest. Third, read the repair bill *before* you pay it. Make sure that you understand all the charges before you pay them. Don't be afraid to ask questions—they can save you money.

Suppose you had to answer this question about the passage:

What is the first thing you should do when you get your TV fixed?

You've read the passage. You may remember the answer to this question. But suppose you didn't remember the first thing to do. How would you answer this question? You would look back at the passage to find the answer.

Would you look back over the whole passage? Or would you do something else? You know something about how the information in the passage is organized. You know that the second part of the passage lists the things to do when you get your TV fixed. You wouldn't have to read the whole passage. You could find the answer by looking back at the second part of the passage. You could *scan* the second part to find the answer.

Getting your TV fixed can cost a lot of money. But there are three things you can do to make sure that you're not paying *too* much money. **First, check to see if the TV is covered by a warranty.** If it is, chances are that you won't have to pay much to get the TV fixed. Second, ask the repair shop to tell you what is wrong with the TV *before* it gets fixed. Ask for an estimate of how much it will cost to have the TV fixed. . . .

Try It: Looking at Organization

Read the next passages. The information in the left-hand column tells you how each passage is organized. Use this information to find the answers to the questions that follow each passage.

1. Closeness of planets to the sun

   There are nine planets in the solar system. The planet that is closest to the sun is Mercury. The second closest planet is Venus. Then comes Earth, Mars, Jupiter, Saturn, Uranus, Neptune, and Pluto.

2. Size of the planets

   Pluto is the farthest planet from the sun. It is also the smallest planet in the solar system. The second smallest planet is Mercury. The other planets in size order are Venus (the third smallest planet), Mars, Earth, Neptune, Uranus, Saturn, and Jupiter.

3. Gravity on the planets

   The planet with the strongest gravity is Jupiter. The planet with the second strongest gravity is Neptune. Then comes Saturn, Uranus, Earth, Venus, and Mars and Mercury. The force of gravity on Pluto is not known.

1. Which planet is closest to the sun?

2. Which planet has the second strongest gravity?

3. What is the third smallest planet?

4. Which of these three planets is the largest?

   (a) Pluto
   (b) Mars
   (c) Saturn

1. Introduction about poison ivy dermatitis

The words "poison ivy" are enough to make a person's skin feel itchy. Poison ivy dermatitis is a rash. And anyone who has suffered from it can tell you that it is a painful rash.

2. How a person gets poison ivy

The poison ivy rash is one of the most common of all allergic skin rashes. Anyone who comes into contact with the sap of poison ivy, poison oak, or poison sumac plants can get the rash. A person doesn't even have to touch the plant to get poison ivy. A person can get the rash just by touching something (such as shoes or clothing) that has come into contact with the plant.

3. Steps for treating poison ivy

There are a lot of medicines that claim to relieve the pain of poison ivy dermatitis. But tests have shown that the best medicine is simple calamine lotion. Experts say that the best way to treat poison ivy is to first apply compresses of cool tap water. The second step is to apply calamine lotion to the rash. The last step is to take some aspirin to help soothe the suffering.

5. What is poison ivy dermatitis?

6. What is the best medicine for treating poison ivy?

7. What are the names of the plants that can give a person poison ivy?

Check your answers on page 43.

ORGANIZING IDEAS AS YOU READ

Knowing how things are put together in a passage can save you time. It can help make it easier to find information that you need. It can really be helpful when a passage contains a lot of information.

For example, read the next passage. As you read, try to keep track of how the information in the passage is organized. You can do this by writing notes in the blanks next to the passage.

1. _____
   _____

      The Liberty Bell is a famous American symbol. It is a symbol of the spirit of the American Revolution. But the history of the Liberty Bell started years before the American Revolution.

      The original Liberty Bell was called the Province Bell. It was made in 1752. It was made to mark the 50th anniversary of the Pennsylvania colony.

2. _____
   _____

      The original Province Bell did not last long. One month after it was made, it cracked. The bell was sent back to be recast, or remade. The first time the bell was recast, it did not work right. Again, it was sent back to be recast. Finally, the bell worked. It was hung in the State House in Philadelphia.

3. _____
   _____

      The Province Bell became known as the Liberty Bell in 1776. It got its name from the fact that it was used to signal the first public reading of the Declaration of Independence. The Declaration of Independence was the document that announced the independence of America from Britain.

4. _____
   _____

      During the Revolutionary War, the Liberty Bell was actually taken out of Philadelphia. In September of 1777, the British Army was ready to invade Philadelphia. Americans didn't want their national symbol to be captured. They took the Liberty Bell out of the State House and moved it to Allentown, Pennsylvania. It stayed in Allentown until June 1778, when the British left Philadelphia.

5. _____
   _____

      If you've ever seen a picture of the Liberty Bell, you probably noticed that the bell is cracked. The crack in the bell appeared in July 1835. The bell cracked when it was tolled to mark the death of John Marshall, the Chief Justice of the Supreme Court.

    Now, cover up the passage about the Liberty Bell with a separate sheet of paper. But don't cover up your notes about how the passage is organized. Then try to answer the following questions. Use your notes to answer the questions.

1. In what part of the story will you find information about the original Province Bell?

2. In what part of the story will you find information about when the crack in the Liberty Bell appeared?

Did your notes help you to answer the questions? Chances are that they did. The questions asked you where you would find certain information in the passage. You made notes on how the information in the passage was organized. For example, you probably mentioned "the Province Bell" in your notes for the second part of the passage. The first question asked you where you would find information about the Province Bell. From your notes, you probably knew that this information was in the second part of the passage.

The second question asked about the crack in the Liberty Bell.

Look at your notes for the fifth part of the passage. What do your notes say? They probably say something about the crack in the Liberty Bell. From your notes, you probably could tell where to find information about when the crack appeared. You could find the information in the fifth part of the passage.

By keeping notes, you were able to tell where to find certain information. You were able to do this without reading the passage a second time. That's because the notes helped you to keep track of the information in the passage. They helped you to keep track of how the passage was organized.

Writing down notes is a good way to keep track of information in a passage. You can use the notes to find the answers to questions about the passage. Notes can make finding the answers a lot faster and a lot easier.

You can practice writing down and using notes on your own. You can do this by cutting stories out of a newspaper. Put each story on a piece of paper. As you read the story, write your notes on the paper. Use the notes to keep track of the information. The more you practice, the easier it will be to write down helpful notes.

Try It: Organizing Ideas as You Read

Read the passages on the next pages. As you read, use the blanks to the left of the passages to write down notes about how the passages are organized. Then try to use your notes to find the answers to the questions that follow each passage.

1. _____
   _____

Iceland is an island country. It is located in the North Atlantic Ocean. Its size is 39,702 square miles, which makes it about the same size as the state of Virginia.

2. _____
   _____

Fewer than 250,000 people live in Iceland. Nearly 90% of these people live in Iceland's cities. About 85,000 people live in the city of Reykjavik, which is Iceland's capital and largest city.

3. _____
   _____

Fishing is a major industry in Iceland. Other major industries of the country are aluminum mining, cement making, and chemical production. Although most of Iceland is wasteland, some farming is done there. The chief crops are potatoes, turnips, and hay.

4. _____
   _____

Iceland's national government is a republic. In the government, the president is the head of state. But the head of the government is the prime minister. In addition to the national government, there are county and municipal governments in Iceland.

1. About how many people live in the city of Reykjavik?

2. In Iceland's government, who is the head of state?

3. What are Iceland's four major industries?

1. _____
   _____

Hector Lopez works in a warehouse. His salary is $250 a week. But he only gets $182.45 of that money. What happens to the rest of Hector's money?

2. _____
   _____

The $250 salary that Hector is supposed to get is called his gross pay. The gross pay is the amount of money that a person makes *before* he pays his taxes. The $182.45 that Hector actually gets is called his net pay. The net pay is the amount of money that a person gets *after* he pays his taxes. The taxes are withheld from his paycheck. This means that the money is taken out before Hector gets his check.

3. _____
   _____

Every week, Hector pays three kinds of taxes. The first tax that Hector pays is the federal withholding tax. The money from this tax goes to pay for the running of the national government. The second tax that Hector pays is called the FICA tax. The money from this tax goes to pay for Social Security and unemployment programs. The third tax that Hector pays is the state withholding tax. The money from this tax goes to pay for the running of the state government.

4. _____   Hector pays a lot of different taxes. But, in a way,
_____   he's lucky. He doesn't live in a city that has a city tax.
Millions of Americans have money taken out of their
paychecks to pay for the running of their city's
government.

4. What does the money from the FICA tax go to pay for?

5. The amount of money that a person makes *before* taxes is called

    (1)   gross pay
    (2)   net pay
    (3)   withholding pay

6. The passage says that Hector Lopez does *not* have to pay one
kind of tax. Which kind of tax doesn't Hector Lopez pay?

    (1)   federal withholding tax
    (2)   FICA tax
    (3)   city withholding tax

Check your answers on page 44.

ANSWERING MULTIPLE-CHOICE QUESTIONS

Take another look at question 6 from the last exercise:

6. The passage says that Hector Lopez does *not* have to
pay one kind of tax. Which kind of tax doesn't Hector
Lopez pay?

    (1)   federal withholding tax
    (2)   FICA tax
    (3)   city withholding tax

This question is an example of a **multiple-choice question**. A
multiple-choice question does two things. First, it asks a question.
Then, it gives a list of answer choices. One of the choices is the correct answer to the question.

Most reading tests are made up of short passages and multiple-choice questions. All the questions on the GED Test are multiple-choice questions. There are strategies that you can use to answer multiple-choice questions. These strategies can help make it easier to answer the questions. Throughout this book, you will find tips on answering multiple-choice questions.

The first step in answering a multiple-choice question is to look at the top part of the question. This top part is called the **stem**. The stem can be a question, such as this one:

The passage says that Hector Lopez does *not* have to pay one kind of tax. Which kind of tax doesn't Hector Lopez pay?

Or, the stem could be a statement that needs an ending:

The amount of money that a person makes *before* taxes is called

The stem is the most important part of a multiple-choice question. The stem gives you the information that you need to find the correct answer.

When you answer a multiple-choice question, make sure that you read the stem *carefully*. It's important that you know exactly what the question is asking. That's because some multiple-choice questions are tricky. Sometimes, it may seem that more than one of the answer choices can be correct. But only *one* of the choices is correct. If you know exactly what the question is asking, you'll have an easier time finding the one correct answer.

Throughout the exercises in this book, you will find multiple-choice questions. Some of the questions will be a little tricky. Use the questions in this book to sharpen your answering skills. The book will also point out some of the tricky kinds of questions that appear on tests like the GED. It will help you to prepare for these kinds of questions.

UNIT REVIEW

In this unit, you've taken a look at how to keep track of ideas in a passage. Keeping track of where ideas are in a passage can be very helpful. It can help you to find information quickly. It can help you to find answers to questions about the passage.

One basic way to keep track of ideas is to write down notes. You can use the notes to point out where information is located in a passage. Notes can be very helpful when you are reading a longer passage that has a lot of information in it.

You can use the things that you read every day to practice writing notes. For example, you can practice writing down notes about a story in the newspaper. The more you practice, the easier it will be to write down helpful notes.

ANSWERS AND EXPLANATIONS

Try It: Looking at Organization

1. **Mercury** is the planet that is closest to the sun. You can find the answer to this question in the first paragraph. In the left-hand column, the first paragraph is labeled "Closeness of planets to the sun."

2. **Neptune** is the planet with the second strongest gravity. You can find the answer to this question in the last paragraph. In the left-hand column, the last paragraph is labeled "Gravity on the planets."

3. **Venus** is the third smallest planet. You can find the answer to this question in the second paragraph. In the left-hand column, the second paragraph is labeled "Size of the planets."

4. **(c)** Of the three planets listed, Saturn is the largest. You can find the answer to this question in the second paragraph. In the left-hand column, the second paragraph is labeled "Size of the planets." The planets are listed in size order, from the smallest to the largest.

5. Poison ivy dermatitis is **a rash**. You can find the answer to this question in the first paragraph. In the left-hand column, the first paragraph is labeled "Introduction about poison ivy dermatitis."

6. The best medicine for treating poison ivy is **simple calamine lotion**. You can find the answer to this question in the last paragraph. In the left-hand column, the last paragraph is labeled "Steps for treating poison ivy."

7. The **poison ivy, poison oak**, and **poison sumac** plants can give a person poison ivy. You can find the answer to this question in the second paragraph. In the left-hand column, the second paragraph is labeled "How a person gets poison ivy."

Try It: Organizing Ideas As You Read

1. About **85,000** people live in the city of Reykjavik. You can find the answer to this question in the second paragraph. The second paragraph contains facts about the population of Iceland.

2. The **president** is the head of state in Iceland's government. You can find the answer to this question in the last paragraph. The last paragraph contains facts about the government of Iceland.

3. **Fishing, aluminum mining, cement making**, and **chemical production** are Iceland's four major industries. You can find the answer to this question in the third paragraph. The third paragraph contains facts about industries in Iceland.

4. The money from the FICA tax goes to pay for **Social Security and unemployment programs**. You can find the answer to this question in the third paragraph. The third paragraph explains the three different taxes that Hector Lopez pays.

5. (1) The amount of money that a person makes *before* taxes is called gross pay. You can find the answer to this question in the second paragraph. In the second paragraph, the terms *gross pay, net pay,* and *withheld* are explained.

6. (3) Hector Lopez doesn't pay a city withholding tax. You can find the answer to this question in the last paragraph.

UNIT 3: USING CLUES TO UNLOCK WORD MEANINGS

RONCHIA

What is this word? What does it mean? Is it the name of a tool that scientists use? Is it the name of a language? Is it something that people do to forget their problems?

You don't know. You don't know because you've never seen this word before. You've never used it.

Look at the word once again:

RONCHIA

There's another reason that you can't tell what the word is. The reason is this: The word is by itself. There are no other words around it. There are no other words to help you guess what the word means. There is no **context** to help you with the word.

A word usually doesn't just appear by itself. Usually, it appears with other words. Together, these words communicate ideas to you. Together, these words form a context. In this unit, you will look at how to use the context to unlock a word's meaning.

WHAT ARE CONTEXT CLUES?

When you read, you may come across words that you don't know. It happens to everyone who reads. You may not know a word if you look at it by itself. But an unknown word is usually in a context. The other words in the context may help you to figure out the unknown word. The other words may provide you with **context clues.**

Using context clues is a reading skill. But it's also a thinking skill. It's a skill that you use all the time, even when you don't read. For example, think about this. Suppose you are listening to the radio. You hear this commercial:

"Introducing the brand new Ronchia! Now, you *can* afford to drive in comfort! The Ronchia has room enough for six people, but it's small enough to get gas mileage that beats the imports! And Ronchia has a price that puts the imports to shame!

"So, get smart! Test-drive a Ronchia today. You'll be glad you did!"

What is a Ronchia? The commercial never really tells you what a Ronchia is. But there are a few clues in the commercial. These clues are context clues. You could use them to figure out what a Ronchia is.

Here are some of the context clues from the commercial:

- Now, you *can* afford to **drive** in comfort!
- The Ronchia has **room enough for six people,** but it's small enough to get **gas mileage** that beats the imports!
- **Test-drive** a Ronchia today.

Each sentence gives you a different context clue. You put the clues together to figure out what a Ronchia is. A Ronchia is a car.

Think back to the beginning of this unit. You saw the word *Ronchia.* You didn't know anything about the word. The word didn't have any context. You couldn't find any clues to help you with the word.

The commercial gave you a context. It gave you clues. The context clues made it easy for you to figure out what a Ronchia is.

Try It: What Are Context Clues?

Here are three more commercials. Use the context clues to figure out what each product is.

"Are your clothes as clean as they should be? If they aren't, try Tring! Tring will make your clothes look better in no time! Your whites will look whiter! Your colors will look brighter!

"So, throw out your old detergents! Get Tring! Your clothes will look like a million dollars!"

1. What is Tring?

"It's 3 P.M. Dinner is hours away. But your body wants something *now*. What should you do?

"Grab a Goggbar! A Goggbar has a chewy center that's loaded with peanuts and covered by thick, creamy chocolate. A Goggbar can give you what you need to get through the day!

"So, keep those hunger pains on hold. Grab a Goggbar today!"

2. What is a Goggbar?

"The next time you have a cough, don't wait. Reach for Romulan 500!

"The ingredients in Romulan 500 will soothe your aching throat and stop your cough. Just two tablespoons of Romulan 500 will give you relief that will last for hours!

"Remember—take Romulan 500, and get rid of your cough!"

3. What is Romulan 500?

Check your answers on page 60.

USING DEFINITIONS AS CONTEXT CLUES

Finding and using context clues when you read is like anything else. Some context clues are easier to find and use than others. For example, look at this paragraph:

There are more than one million types of animals in the world. But all these animals can be divided into two main groups—vertebrates and invertebrates. Vertebrates are animals that have a backbone. Invertebrates are animals that do not have a backbone.

What are vertebrates? What are invertebrates?

You can use context clues in the paragraph to answer these questions. The context clues are pretty easy to find. They are in the last two sentences of the paragraph.

Vertebrates are animals that have a backbone.

Invertebrates are animals that do not have a backbone.

The sentences tell you what the words mean. They give you **definitions** of the words.

A definition is the easiest kind of context clue to find and use. If you have a definition, you don't have to guess what the word means. The definition tells you.

The definitions of the words *vertebrates* and *invertebrates* were easy to spot. In each sentence, the word *are* points to the definition. Most of the time, it's easy to spot a definition. But sometimes it's a little harder. For example, look at this paragraph:

Last week, Jack felt pains in his chest. He went to his doctor for a checkup. His doctor gave him some tests. Then the doctor sent Jack to a cardiologist, a doctor who treats heart diseases.

What is a cardiologist?

The word *cardiologist* is defined in the paragraph. The definition might be a little hard to find at first. That's because there aren't any words that point to the definition. The definition is in the last sentence of the paragraph:

Then the doctor sent Jack to a cardiologist, <u>a doctor who</u> <u>treats heart diseases</u>.

The definition comes right after the word *cardiologist*. But there isn't any word that points to the definition. There's only a comma between the word and the definition. You have to look at the way the sentence is put together to find the definition.

Try It: Using Definitions As Context Clues

Read each paragraph. Then look at the words below the paragraph. Find the definition of each word in the paragraph. Then put the definition on the line next to the word.

Meteorologists are people who study weather. They use many different kinds of tools in their work. One tool that they use is a barometer, an instrument that measures air pressure. Another tool that meteorologists use is an anemometer. An anemometer is an instrument that measures the speed of wind.

1. meteorologists:_____

2. barometer:_____

3. anemometer:_____

      Getting a bank loan isn't easy. A borrower has to prove that he can pay the money back. He has to have collateral, property that can be sold to pay back the loan. Sometimes, the borrower needs a cosigner for the loan. A cosigner is a person who signs for the loan along with the borrower. If the borrower can't pay back the loan, the bank can force the cosigner to pay back the money.

4. collateral:_____

5. cosigner:_____

Check your answers on page 60.

USING EXAMPLES AS CONTEXT CLUES

      Definitions are the easiest kind of context clue to use. The definition usually tells you exactly what the word means. But definitions are only one kind of context clue. There are others. For example, look at this paragraph:

      Doctors have made great progress in treating and curing many serious illnesses. However, they have been unable to find ways to prevent the most common illnesses. It seems that such maladies as colds, fevers, and sore throats will always be a part of life.

      What are maladies?

      You won't find a definition of the word *maladies* in the paragraph. But there are some clues that you can use to figure out what maladies are.

      The first clue is in the sentence in which the word appears:

It seems that such maladies as colds, fevers, and sore
throats will always be a part of life.

The sentence gives you three examples of maladies. The examples are colds, fevers, and sore throats. You know that colds, fevers,
and sore throats are kinds of illnesses. From this, you can guess that
maladies are illnesses.

There's another clue that can help you to figure this out. What is
the paragraph mainly about? The paragraph is mainly about illnesses. The first two sentences are about illnesses. The last sentence
is about maladies. The main idea of the paragraph gives you the clue
that maladies are illnesses.

Think about the two context clues that you just used. Neither
clue told you exactly what the word *maladies* means. However, each
clue gave you a piece of information. You used the information to
figure out something about the word *maladies*.

Most of the context clues that you will find will only give you
pieces of information. It's up to you to put the pieces together. Some
clues will be easier to find than others. Some clues will be more helpful than others. You may have found the examples of maladies a
helpful clue. Or you may have found it easier to use the main idea of
the paragraph to figure out what maladies are. When you come
across a word that you don't know, find as many context clues as you
can. Each clue will give you another piece of information to use.

Examples are usually an easy context clue to find. But sometimes they are a little harder to spot. For example, look at this paragraph:

Senator Tom Hanks is from an area where the
unemployment rate is high. The area has many factories
that have closed down in the past few years. The
senator thinks that he has the answer to the area's
unemployment problem. He wants the U.S. government to
buy the closed factories. He wants the government to use
the factories to make armaments. He says that America
could use the guns, tanks, and other weapons the
factories would make. He knows that the people in the
area could use the jobs.

What are armaments?

Examples of armaments are given in the paragraph. But the examples may be a little hard to find. The examples appear in a different sentence from the word *armaments*.

He wants the government to use the factories to make armaments. He says that America could use the guns, tanks and other weapons the factories would make.

Guns, tanks, and other weapons are examples of armaments. The paragraph doesn't really tell you this. You have to figure it out. You figure it out by looking at how the ideas in the sentences fit together. The first sentence says that the factories would make armaments. The second sentence says that America could use the guns, tanks, and other weapons that the factories would make. The factories would make armaments. They would make guns, tanks, and other weapons. You can guess that guns, tanks, and other weapons are examples of armaments. You can guess that armaments are weapons.

Examples don't tell you exactly what a word means. But they *can* give you some good clues to a word's meaning. Examples can help you to figure out something about a word that you don't know.

Try It: Using Examples As Context Clues

Read each paragraph. Then answer the questions that follow the paragraph.

Fixing a broken table or shelf isn't fun. But it's usually cheaper than buying new furniture. One key to doing the job right is having the right tools. Such implements as a hammer, a screwdriver, and pliers will make it much easier to do the job the right way.

1. The paragraph gives three examples of implements. What are the three examples?

2. What are implements?

Carl J. Argon has a strange hobby. He likes to climb buildings. But he doesn't use the stairs inside the building. Instead, he climbs buildings on the outside. Argon has climbed many small buildings, as well as a few very big ones. Among the major edifices he has climbed are the 22-story First National Tower Building in Akron, Ohio, and the 28-floor World Trade Center Building in Baltimore.

3. The paragraph gives two examples of edifices. What are the two examples?

4. What are edifices?

Check your answers on page 61.

USING RESTATEMENTS AS CONTEXT CLUES

Definitions and examples are two important kinds of context clues. Another kind of context clue is a **restatement.** Read the next paragraph:

Max was mad at his friend Harry. A month ago, Max lent Harry fifty dollars. Yesterday, Harry paid Max back. He gave Max a check for fifty dollars. Max took the check to the bank. He tried to cash it. But the bank wouldn't cash the check. The teller said the check couldn't be cashed because of "insufficient funds." In other words, there wasn't enough money in Harry's bank account to pay the check.

What does *"insufficient funds"* mean?

The answer to this question is in the last two sentences of the paragraph.

The teller said the check couldn't be cashed because of "insufficient funds." In other words, there wasn't enough money in Harry's bank account to pay the check.

The last sentence begins with *in other words*. The rest of the sentence tells you what *"insufficient funds"* means. It tells you what it means by using other words. It is a restatement of the words *"insufficient funds."* There wasn't enough money in Harry's bank account to pay the check. You can figure out that *"insufficient funds"* means "not enough money."

The phrase *in other words* tells you that a context clue is coming up. It points to a restatement. The phrase makes it easier to find the context clue. But sometimes the phrase isn't used. For example, look at this story:

Last week, something happened to Roger White. It's something that has happened to many Americans in recent years.

About six months ago, Roger White bought a brand-new car. He got a loan from a loan company to pay for the car. Roger had a hard time paying back the loan. Last month, Roger defaulted on his loan. He could not meet his monthly payment.

The loan company acted quickly. Last week, the company sent two men to Roger's house. The two men repossessed Roger's new car. They took the car away from Roger.

What does *defaulted* mean? What does *repossessed* mean?

The meanings of both of these words are restated in the story. But there aren't any phrases that point to the restatements. Take another look at these two sentences:

Last month, Roger defaulted on his loan. He could not meet his monthly payment.

The first sentence tells you that Roger defaulted on his loan. The second sentence says the same thing, but in different words. It tells you that he could not meet his monthly payments. From the restatement, you can figure out what *defaulted* means. It means "not meeting a payment on a loan."

Now, look at these two sentences. From the restatement, can you tell what *repossessed* means?

The two men repossessed Roger's new car. They took the car away from Roger.

The second sentence restates the meaning of the first sentence. It uses other words to tell you what the first sentence means. The men repossessed the car. They took it away. You can figure out that *repossessed* means "took away."

A restatement can often give you a good clue to the meaning of a word. Some restatements are easy to spot. Such words and phrases as *in other words* and *that is* point to restatements. Some restatements are harder to find. They don't have any words or phrases that point to them. But, if you can find them, they can be very helpful.

Try It: Using Restatements As Context Clues

Read each story. Then answer the questions that follow the story.

A year ago, the Abington Phillies football team was torn apart by dissension. Players openly fought with one another, and the head coach threatened to beat up the team's quarterback. The reason for the fighting was that the team was stuck in last place. This year, however, things are different. The Phillies have a winning record, and it looks as though they will make the playoffs.

What has caused the sudden turnaround in the team? Coach Lou Zola thinks he knows the answer to this question. "I think that all the fighting last year revitalized us," he said. "In other words, the club was stuck in a rut. The fighting gave us a new life. It gave us a new outlook on things."

1. Which of the following words means nearly the same thing as *dissension?*

   (1) threatened
   (2) fighting
   (3) winning

2. Which of the following is the best definition of the word *revitalized?*

   (1) stuck in a rut
   (2) a new life
   (3) outlook on things

Roland Cleves is a mercenary. That is, he's a professional soldier who will fight for whoever is willing to pay him. In the last ten years, Cleves has fought wars in South America and Africa. He says that he does it because "the pay is good and I like my job."

Cleves says that he has no qualms about being a mercenary. "I don't have any guilt feelings at all," he says. "After all, wars are going to be fought whether or not I fight in them. People will die whether I shoot them or someone else does."

3. What is a mercenary?

4. What are qualms?

Check your answers on page 61.

USING OPPOSITES AS CONTEXT CLUES

The context clues that you've looked at so far can help you by telling you what a word means. But here's a kind of context clue that helps you in a different way. It helps you by telling you what a word does *not* mean.

Fred and Mel Blode are twins. But they are as different from each other as two people can be. Fred is very boisterous. Mel is just the opposite; he's very quiet. Fred likes to spend his money. On the other hand, Mel is frugal. Fred is usually a cheerful person; however, Mel is usually sullen.

What does *boisterous* mean?

What does *frugal* mean?

What does *sullen* mean?

There are context clues in the paragraph to help you to figure out what these words mean. But the clues don't tell you what the words mean. Instead, they tell you what the words *don't* mean. They give you the **opposites** of the words.

Here is the context clue for the word *boisterous:*

Fred is very boisterous. Mel is just the opposite; he's very quiet.

What does *boisterous* mean? From the context clue, you can tell that it means the opposite of *quiet.* From the context clue, you can figure out that *boisterous* must mean "loud."

Opposites are an important kind of context clue. They are a little harder to use because they don't give you a word's meaning. Instead, they give you the opposite of the word's meaning. You figure out what the word means from the opposite meaning that's given.

Here are the words *frugal* and *sullen* with their context clues. Can you use the clues to figure out what the words mean?

Fred likes to spend his money. On the other hand, Mel is very frugal. Fred is usually a cheerful person; however, Mel is usually sullen.

Look at the first two sentences again. The words *on the other hand* tell you that Mel is the opposite of Fred. Fred likes to spend his money. Mel is frugal. He is the opposite of Fred. You can figure out that a frugal person is a person who does not like to spend money.

Now, look at the last sentence again. The word *however* again tells you that Mel is the opposite of Fred. Fred is usually cheerful. Mel is usually sullen. You can guess that *sullen* means "not cheerful."

Such words as *however, on the other hand, instead,* and *but* point to opposites. Sometimes, you can use opposites to figure out the meaning of a word that you don't know. Opposites can be a very helpful kind of context clue.

Try It: Using Opposites as Context Clues

Read each story. Then answer the questions that follow the story.

Frank Fernandez used to be the most talkative player on the team. Reporters would always look for Frank after a big game because he always had something to say. But Frank Fernandez has changed over the years. Now, Fernandez is laconic. No one knows what has caused the big change in his behavior.

1. Which word means nearly the same thing as *laconic*?

    (1) happy
    (2) quiet
    (3) funny

Harriet Grimsley is a woman with a cause. She wants to bring back the good old days.

Harriet is the president of a society. The society is called "People for the Past," or PFP for short. The society is made up of people like Harriet. They want to bring back the things that they liked about the past.

Exactly what does Harriet Grimsley like about the past? "For one thing, I want us to go back to our old values," she said recently. "In the old days, people respected one another. But today, too many people are downright insolent."

Harriet and her society also want to see other changes. They feel that life today is too bewildering; they'd like to return to a simpler way of life.

"Modern society has changed people a lot, and most of the changes are not good," Harriet Grimsley said. "People used to care about one another. But TV has changed all that. Now, most people are very insensitive to others. We'd like to try to change that."

2. Which word means nearly the same thing as *insolent*?

    (1) rude
    (2) young
    (3) poor

3. Which word means nearly the same thing as *bewildering*?

    (1) confusing
    (2) sickening
    (3) comforting

4. Which word means nearly the same thing as *insensitive*?

    (1) lazy
    (2) quiet
    (3) uncaring

Check your answers on page 62.

UNIT REVIEW

In this unit, you've worked with **context clues.** Context clues are words, phrases, or sentences that you can use to figure out the meaning of a word that you don't know.

You've worked with four different kinds of context clues in this unit. You've worked with using **definitions, examples, restatements,** and **opposites** as context clues. Some context clues are easier to use than others. For example, a definition is an easy kind of context clue to use. A definition tells you exactly what a word means. An example is a context clue that is a little harder to use. You have to figure out what a word means from some examples that are given.

Context clues aren't always easy to use. But they are important to use when you read. They can help you to unlock the meanings of words that you don't know. They can help make reading a little easier for you.

The next exercise will give you a chance to practice using all the different kinds of context clues that you worked with in this unit.

Try It: Using Context Clues

Read the next passage. Then answer the questions that follow the passage.

What does it take to be a master chef? Dusty Taub thinks he knows the answer. For 17 years, Dusty has cooked thousands of meals at his restaurant, "Dusty's Place." Now, Dusty is sharing his secrets with anyone who cares to hear them. He's put all his cooking hints in a new book. The book is called *Filling the Plate.*

Dusty got his start as a chef early in life. By the time he was 17, he'd been trained as a saucier, a chef who specializes in making sauces and soups. He graduated from the Columbia School of Culinary Arts when he was 22. Two years later, he opened "Dusty's Place."

Dusty says that the secret to good cooking is in preparing for a meal. "You have to prepare everything carefully," he says. "You can't do it haphazardly. You have to be meticulous. I mean, you *really* have to be careful."

Dusty serves up such victuals as barbecued ribs, roast duck, and steamed lobster at his restaurant. He has created such dishes as "Veal a la Dusty" and "Chicken in Pea Sauce." But Dusty's favorite food is hamburger. "It's simple, and it tastes great," he says.

1. Which word means nearly the same thing as *haphazardly*?

   (1) carefully
   (2) carelessly
   (3) secretly

2. Which word means nearly the same thing as *meticulous*?

   (1) careful
   (2) careless
   (3) secret

3. Which word means nearly the same thing as *victuals*?

   (1) wines
   (2) restaurants
   (3) meals

4. What is a saucier?

Read the next passage. Then look at the lists of words that follow the passage. In the blanks before the left-hand column, fill in the letters of the word or words in the right-hand column that mean nearly the same thing.

One of the oldest types of winged insects is the cockroach. Throughout history, wherever people have built homes, cockroaches have shared the space. There is no way to assess, or make a judgment about, the exact number of cockroaches, but current studies show that today's population is huge. This is because cockroaches are so tough. They can live as long as two months without food or water. When they do eat, they are omnivorous. They consume food, paper, books, clothing—almost anything! On top of this, they are prolific breeders. The female roach has about 16 babies every five days.

In order to control the cockroach population, scientists are working on new types of roach traps. One of the latest traps attracts cockroaches through the use of pheromones. Pheromones are chemicals formed by insects that affect the behavior of other insects. Scientists can now create fake sex pheromones. These copy the odor that cockroaches use to attract each other. Traps that use these fake pheromones have been shown to work better than traps that use food.

5. _____ prolific   a. chemicals

6. _____ assess   b. able to eat anything

7. _____ pheromones   c. make a judgment

8. _____ omnivorous   d. producing many young

Check your answers on page 62.

ANSWERS AND EXPLANATIONS

Try It: What Are Context Clues?

1. Tring is **a brand of laundry detergent.** The commercial tells you that Tring can make your clothes look better. It tells you to throw out your old detergents and get Tring. From these clues, you can figure out that Tring is a laundry detergent.

2. A Goggbar is **a kind of candy bar.** The commercial describes a Goggbar. It says that a Goggbar has a chewy center that's loaded with peanuts and covered by chocolate. From this description, you can tell that a Goggbar is a candy bar.

3. Romulan 500 is **a kind of cough medicine.** The commercial tells you to take Romulan 500 to get rid of your cough. It tells you that two tablespoons of Romulan 500 will give you relief. From this, you can tell that Romulan 500 is a cough medicine.

Try It: Using Definitions as Context Clues

1. Meteorologists are **people who study weather.** The word *meteorologists* is defined in the first sentence of the paragraph.

2. A barometer is **an instrument that measures air pressure.** The definition of *barometer* follows after the word is used in the third sentence.

3. An anemometer is **an instrument that measures the speed of wind.** The word *anemometer* is defined in the last sentence of the paragraph.

4. Collateral is **property that can be sold to pay back a loan.** The word *collateral* is defined in the third sentence of the paragraph. The definition follows the word in the sentence.

5. A cosigner is **a person who signs for a loan along with the borrower.** The word *cosigner* is defined in the fifth sentence of the paragraph.

Try It: Using Examples as Context Clues

1. **A hammer, a screwdriver,** and **pliers** are the three examples of implements given in the paragraph.

2. From the examples, you can figure out that implements are **tools.** A hammer, a screwdriver, and pliers are three kinds of tools.

3. The two examples of edifices given in the paragraph are **the First National Tower Building in Akron, Ohio,** and **the World Trade Center Building in Baltimore.**

4. From the two examples, you can figure out that edifices are **buildings.** The two examples given are both buildings.

Try It: Using Restatements as Context Clues

1. **(2)** "Fighting" means nearly the same thing as *dissension*. The first sentence of the passage tells you that the team was torn apart by dissension. The second sentence restates this by saying that the players and coach fought with one another. From the restatement, you can tell that *dissension* most nearly means "fighting."

2. **(2)** The best definition for *revitalized* is "a new life." The clue for this is in the second paragraph. The coach said that the fighting revitalized the team. The fighting gave the team a new life.

3. A mercenary is **a professional soldier who will fight for whoever is willing to pay him.** The first sentence tells you that Roland Cleves is a mercenary. The second sentence gives a restatement that tells what a mercenary is.

4. From the second paragraph, you can guess that qualms are **guilt feelings.** The first sentence of the paragraph tells you that Cleves has no qualms about his job. He restates this by saying that he doesn't have any guilt feelings.

Try It: Using Opposites as Context Clues

1. **(2)** The word *quiet* means nearly the same thing as *laconic*. The first part of the paragraph tells you that Frank Fernandez used to be talkative. But he's changed. Now, he's laconic. You can guess that *laconic* is the opposite of *talkative*. *Quiet* is the opposite of *talkative*.

2. **(1)** The word *rude* means nearly the same thing as *insolent*. The clue for this is in the third paragraph. Harriet Grimsley said that people used to respect one another. But now they're insolent. You can guess that *insolent* is the opposite of *respectful*.

3. **(1)** The word *confusing* means nearly the same thing as *bewildering*. The clue for this is in the fourth paragraph. Harriet Grimsley said that life today is too bewildering and that she wants to return to a simpler way of life. From this, you can guess that *bewildering* is the opposite of *simple*.

4. **(3)** The word *uncaring* means nearly the same thing as *insensitive*. The clue for this is in the last paragraph. Harriet Grimsley said that people used to care for one another, but now they're insensitive. You can guess that *insensitive* means the opposite of "caring."

Try It: Using Context Clues

1. **(2)** The word *carelessly* means nearly the same thing as *haphazardly*. The clue for this is in the third paragraph. Dusty says that you have to prepare everything carefully. You can't do it haphazardly. You can guess that *haphazardly* means the opposite of "carefully."

2. **(1)** The word *careful* means nearly the same thing as *meticulous*. The clue for this is in the third paragraph. Dusty says, "You have to be meticulous. I mean, you *really* have to be careful." You can guess that the second sentence is a restatement of the first sentence and that *meticulous* means "careful."

3. **(3)** You can guess that *meals* means nearly the same thing as *victuals*. The clue for this is in the last paragraph. Three examples of victuals are given: barbecued ribs, roast duck, and steamed lobster. These are all foods. From the examples, you can figure out that victuals are meals.

4. A saucier is **a chef who specializes in making sauces and soups.** The word *saucier* is defined in the second paragraph. The definition appears after the word *saucier* appears in the second sentence of the paragraph.

5. __d__ *Producing many young* means nearly the same thing as *prolific*. In the next-to-last sentence of the first paragraph, the writer says that cockroaches are prolific breeders. The next sentence then says that female roaches have about 16 babies every five days. That is a lot of babies produced in a short amount of time. From this, you can figure out that *prolific* and *producing many young* mean nearly the same thing.

6. __c__ *Make a judgment* means nearly the same thing as *assess*. The clue for this comes right after the word *assess* in the third sentence. The phrase *or make a judgment about* tells you that this is a restatement of the word *assess*.

7. __a__ *Chemicals* means nearly the same thing as *pheromones*. In the second paragraph, the writer states that pheromones are chemicals that are formed by insects.

8. __b__ *Able to eat anything* means nearly the same thing as *omnivorous*. In the first paragraph, the writer says that when cockroaches eat, they are omnivorous. The next sentence provides an example of the kinds of things cockroaches eat. The writer says that cockroaches eat almost anything. From this, you can figure out that to be omnivorous means to eat almost anything.

Reading for Information

The main reason people read is to get information. You read a newspaper to find out what is going on in the world. You read a set of directions to find out how to use something. You read a recipe to find out how to make a certain kind of dish.

In this section you will take a look at reading for information. In Unit 4 you will work on finding the main idea of a reading passage. In Unit 5 you will work on ways to get details from a reading passage.

At the end of each of the units in this section, you will find a special **Close-up** feature. In the Close-ups you will take a look at some important words and ideas from and about science, social studies, and literature. The Close-ups will help you to build your knowledge of those three subjects.

UNIT 4: FINDING THE MAIN IDEA

Think back to the first section of this book. In Unit 1, you worked on three things. You worked on using previewing, scanning, and predicting when you read. Previewing, scanning, and predicting are important processes in reading. They're important for one main reason. They can help you to find the main idea of a reading passage. In this unit, you'll work on finding the main idea of a reading passage.

WHAT IS THE MAIN IDEA?

The term "main idea" pretty much explains itself. The main idea of a passage is the main thing that a passage says. It's the main point that a passage makes.

In Unit 1 of this book, you worked on previewing, scanning, and predicting. Previewing and scanning can help you to find the topic of a passage. The topic is the subject of a passage. But the topic is *not* the main idea. It is only a part of the main idea. The main idea is a statement about the topic. It is the main thing that the passage says about the topic.

When you worked on predicting, you worked on finding the main idea. In predicting, you try to guess what the passage will say about the topic. You try to guess the main point that the passage will make. In other words, you try to figure out the passage's main idea.

Read the following passage, in which a woman describes her job. Think about what the main idea of the passage is.

Jean Stanley

I sell cosmetics to women who are trying to look young.
They are spending more on treatment creams than they did
years ago. I can remember when lipsticks at two dollars
was tops. Now they have lipsticks that sell for five. Many
times I think, thirty dollars for a little jar of cream. I know
that it doesn't have that value. But in the eye of that
woman, it has that value.
A cosmetic came out that was supposed to smooth out
wrinkles for five or six hours. It puffs out the skin. The
wrinkles would return. We criticized it. But a woman came
in one morning, she said, "I'm going for a job interview and
I'm past forty. I want to look nicer." I feel differently about
selling it to her. It might bring her a job.

The passage is about the work a woman, Jean Stanley, does. She is the topic of the passage. What is the main thing Jean Stanley does in the passage? She sells cosmetics to women who want to look young. The main idea is given in the first sentence.

Look for the main idea in this science passage:

All living things are made of cells. Some tiny plants and animals are made of only one cell. The human body is made of more than a trillion cells. Cells come in different sizes and shapes. Most cells are very small. You have to use a microscope to see them. But some cells are larger. For example, the yolk of an egg is one cell. The shape of a cell usually depends on the cell's function. In the human body, muscle cells are long and thin. Blood cells are round. Nerve cells are long and have many "branches." Messages are sent to different parts of the body through the branches.

What is the topic of this passage?

What is the main idea of this passage?

The answer to the first question is pretty easy. From scanning, you could probably tell that the passage is about cells. The word *cells* appears a number of times. The topic of the passage is cells.

What is the main thing that the passage says about cells? What is the passage's main idea? The passage gives you details about cells. It tells you that cells have different sizes and shapes. But all of the details in the passage support one main idea. They support the idea that all living things are made of cells. This is the main idea of the passage. The first sentence of the passage gives you the main idea.

Now look for the main idea in this excerpt from a biography.

The Indian guides were certain that Alexander Mackenzie was under the control of demons. How else could they explain his endless energy, his daring, his curiosity, his total lack of fear? It was the spring of 1792, and Mackenzie was exploring the Canadian wilds. He was searching for the Northwest Passage—a waterway from the Atlantic to the Pacific Ocean. A madman, they thought. But what strange madness. The guides were proud of their own strength and endurance. They often paddled their canoes 18 hours a day or marched all day and most of the night through the wilderness. But they needed at least a few hours' rest in each 24. Mackenzie, apparently, needed none at all.

What is the topic of this passage?

What is the main idea of this passage?

Alexander Mackenzie is the topic of the passage. You can tell this by scanning the passage. Mackenzie's name is repeated several times, and there are many other references to him. What is the main thing that the passage says about Mackenzie? The passage gives you details about Mackenzie. It tells you about his energy, strength, daring, and curiosity. But all of these details support the idea that the Indian guides were certain that Mackenzie was under the control of demons. The main idea is stated in the first sentence of the passage.

Try It: What Is the Main Idea?

Here are three more reading passages. Before you read each passage, scan it. Try to figure out what the passage's topic is. Then read each passage and answer the questions that follow it.

The national government of the United States is divided into three branches. The branches are called the legislative, the executive, and the judicial. Each branch has separate powers and responsibilities. The legislative branch is called Congress. Congress includes the Senate and the House of Representatives. Congress can make laws and declare war. The executive branch includes the President and his advisers. The executive branch enforces the laws. The President is also the commander-in-chief of the armed forces. The judicial branch is headed by the Supreme Court. The Supreme Court can decide whether a law is allowed by the United States Constitution. The Constitution is the set of rules the government must follow.

1. What is the topic of this passage?

2. What is the main idea of this passage?

"Magic bullets" are a new way to fight disease. "Magic bullets" are not really bullets. They are a special kind of antibody. An antibody attacks germs or other cells that do not belong in the body. Normally, antibodies are made by blood cells. But blood cells make many different kinds of antibodies at once. Some of the antibodies will work against a particular disease. Some of them will not. The "magic bullets" are made in a laboratory. Every cell in a batch of "magic bullets" is exactly alike. This means they can work together better on a particular disease. "Magic bullets" multiply quickly, too. They can stop a disease much faster than normal antibodies.

3. What is the topic of this passage?

4. What is the main idea of this passage?

Cancer is a disease of the body's cells. Cancer cells reproduce too quickly. They get out of control. Then they take away food and oxygen from normal cells. The normal cells die. Scientists say even normal cells have cancer genes. A cancer gene can make a cell reproduce too quickly. Normally, cancer genes are "turned off." But radiation, cigarette smoke, and other things can "turn on" a cancer gene. Then the normal cell gets out of control. It becomes a cancer cell. Scientists are studying cancer genes. They hope there is a way to keep them turned off.

5. What is the topic of this passage?

6. What is the main idea of this passage?

Check your answers on page 78.

DIGGING FOR THE MAIN IDEA

So far in this unit, you've worked on one kind of reading passage. You've worked on passages that begin with a main idea sentence. A main idea sentence tells you exactly what the main idea is.

Most newspaper stories begin with a main idea sentence. The sentence tells you the main thing that the story is about. Some reading passages also begin with a main idea sentence. But be careful. The first sentence of a passage doesn't always give you the main idea. For example, look at this passage:

Suppose the President wants to create a new law. Can he do it by himself? The answer is that he can't. Congress must approve all laws. But Congress can't pass laws by itself, either. The President has the power to veto, or reject, any law that Congress passes. A vetoed bill can become a law only if two-thirds of Congress supports it on a second voting. And the Supreme Court can knock down any law that violates the United States

Constitution. This system of enacting laws is known as
the system of checks and balances. The system of checks
and balances ensures that no one branch of the
government becomes too powerful. It forces the branches
of government to work together.

What is the topic of this passage?

What is the main idea of this passage?

From scanning, you could guess that the topic has something to
do with the President and Congress. As you began to read, you probably figured out that the passage is about how the President and
Congress pass laws. The passage tells you that the government has a
system for passing laws. The system is known as the system of
checks and balances.

What does the passage say about the system of checks and balances? What is the main idea of the passage? You can't get the main
idea from the first sentence. The first sentence really doesn't tell you
what the passage is about. You have to read on to figure out the
main idea. The main idea is hard to figure out until you get to the
end of the passage.

This system of enacting laws is known as the system of
checks and balances. The system of checks and balances
ensures that no one branch of the government becomes
too powerful. It forces the branches of government to
work together.

The main idea of the passage is this: The system of checks and
balances ensures that no one branch of the government becomes too
powerful. The passage does have a main idea sentence. But it's not
the first sentence of the passage. It's near the end of the passage.

The way to find the main idea of a passage is to think about
what the passage is saying. A reading passage is made up of details.
The details have something in common. They all support one main
idea. They all add information to the main idea.

Try It: Digging for the Main Idea

Read the two passages on the next page. Before you read each passage, scan it. Try to figure out what the passage's topic is. Then read
each passage and answer the questions that follow it.

It's easy to think of Congress as one group. But Congress is divided into two bodies, the Senate and the House of Representatives. The Senate is made up of 100 senators, or 2 senators from each state. The House of Representatives is made up of 435 representatives. Each state has at least 1 representative in the House. But the overall number of representatives that a state has depends on the state's population. States that have more people have more representatives.

1. What is the topic of this passage?

2. Which statement from the passage best gives the main idea?

   (1) It's easy to think of Congress as one group.
   (2) Congress is divided into two bodies, the Senate and the House of Representatives.
   (3) The overall number of representatives that a state has depends on the state's population.

Plant cells and animal cells have many things in common. For example, both plant and animal cells have a nucleus. They both have chromosomes and genes. But plant cells are different from animal cells because they have a cell wall and chloroplasts. The cell wall surrounds the plant cell. It gives the plant cell a tough outer covering. Chloroplasts are located in the plant cell. Chloroplasts are very important. They allow plants to produce their own food. All green plants contain chloroplasts.

3. What is the topic of this passage?

4. Which statement from the passage best gives the main idea?

   (1) Plant cells and animal cells have many things in common.
   (2) Chloroplasts are very important.
   (3) Plant cells are different from animal cells because they have a cell wall and chloroplasts.

Check your answers on page 78.

ANSWERING MAIN IDEA QUESTIONS

In the GED tests, you will find main idea questions. The last exercise has examples of one kind of main idea question. Take another look at that kind of question.

Which statement from the passage best gives the main idea?

(1) It's easy to think of Congress as one group.
(2) Congress is divided into two bodies, the Senate and the House of Representatives.
(3) The overall number of representatives that a state has depends on the state's population.

In this kind of question, you have to choose a main idea sentence. One of the sentences gives the main idea. The other two do not.

The best way to answer a question like this one is to first read the passage. See if you can figure out the passage's main idea. Then read each answer choice for the question. Choose the answer that best gives the main idea.

Read the next passage. Then answer the question that follows it.

Why do some people have light hair and some dark hair? Why do children often look like their parents? The answers to questions like these can be found in genes. Genes give a living thing its special features. They are contained in the nucleus of cells. Genes are made up of a substance called DNA. Each gene contains a "message." The message controls a certain characteristic of the living thing. In human cells, there are genes for such characteristics as sex, hair color, eye color, and height.

Which statement from the passage best gives the main idea?

(1) Genes give a living thing its special features.
(2) Genes are made up of a substance called DNA.
(3) Each gene contains a "message."

Look at the three answer choices to the question. Each answer choice is a sentence from the passage. Which sentence is the main idea sentence?

The topic of the passage is genes. The main purpose of the passage is to answer the two questions that begin the passage. Therefore, the main idea should be an answer to the two questions. The main idea is that genes give a living thing its special features. Answer choice 1 is the correct answer.

Take one more look at choices 2 and 3. Why aren't they correct? Answer choice 2 tells you that genes are made up of a substance called DNA. This fact is stated in the passage. But the whole passage does not discuss what genes are made of. Only a small part of the passage discusses this. Answer choice 2 is too specific. Answer choice 3 tells you that each gene contains a "message." The passage says this. But what is the message? Why is the message important? Answer choice 3 doesn't tell you this. It doesn't give you enough information to be the main idea sentence.

Whenever you answer a main idea question, remember this. A main idea is made up of two basic parts. First, a main idea tells the topic of a passage. Second, a main idea tells the main thing that the passage says about the topic. The answer to a main idea question should not be too general. It shouldn't just give the topic of the passage. On the other hand, it should not be too specific, either. It shouldn't give only one small detail from the passage.

Try It: Answering Main Idea Questions

Here are three more reading passages. Read each passage, and then answer the questions that follow it.

In 1969, when Richard Nixon came into office, he showed no great interest in pulling out of Vietnam. In Congress, however, a growing number of legislators were opposed to the war. But because of a peculiar voting system in the House of Representatives, it was all too easy for members to sit on the fence. Under the rules of the House, members voting on amendments would walk down one of the two aisles of the House—depending on whether they were voting yea or nay. When they reached the front of the line, they were tapped on the shoulder by a teller—a fellow representative who was counting votes. The final vote would be recorded, but . . . it was almost impossible to know how—or even if—an individual member had voted.

1. Which of the following is the topic of the passage?

(1) Richard Nixon
(2) Congress
(3) a voting procedure used in the House of Representatives
(4) opposition to the Vietnam war

2. Which of the following statements best gives the main idea of the passage?

   (1)   In Congress, a growing number of legislators were opposed to the war.

   (2)   Because of a peculiar voting system in the House of Representatives, it was all too easy for members to sit on the fence.

   (3)   Richard Nixon showed no great interest in pulling out of Vietnam.

   (4)   Members voting on amendments would walk down one of the two aisles of the House.

       The cosmetics sold to women come at a price—a price in suffering that few are aware of. To be certain that the cosmetics are safe, manufacturers are required to test them, on rabbits' eyes.

       The suffering and blindness caused by the tests have infuriated people fighting for animals' rights. And cosmetic manufacturers, too, dislike the tests which, in addition to being inhuman, are expensive.

       A recent development, called "Test Skin," may solve the problems of cosmetic testing. "Test Skin" is a kind of complicated cell growth made in the laboratory. It acts remarkably like human skin. It is not part of a living creature. And tests using it cost only one-tenth the amount of tests using rabbits.

       Many scientists are hopeful that "Test Skin," or something like it, will someday bring an end to the cruel and needless suffering rabbits undergo in cosmetic testing laboratories.

3. Which of the following is the topic of the passage?

   (1)   cosmetics
   (2)   rabbits
   (3)   cosmetic testing
   (4)   "Test Skin"

4. Which of the following statements best gives the main idea of the passage?

   (1)   Many people are upset about the suffering rabbits undergo in cosmetic testing.

   (2)   Cosmetic manufacturers dislike tests that use rabbits, partly because such tests are very expensive.

(3) A laboratory product, "Test Skin," may solve the problems of cruelty and expense in cosmetic testing.

(4) "Test Skin," which is made in the laboratory, is a complicated cell growth remarkably like human skin.

The Constitution is the main law of the United States. The Constitution says that the President of the United States must be at least 35 years old. Suppose people wanted to change this law. How could it be changed? Could Congress change it? Could the President change it?

The only way that the Constitution can be changed is through an amendment. The word *amendment* means "change." Congress cannot pass an amendment. The President cannot order an amendment. An amendment to the Constitution can only be made if two things happen. First, two thirds of both the Senate and the House of Representatives must approve the amendment. Second, three fourths of the state governments must ratify, or approve, the amendment.

5. Which of the following is the topic of the passage?

   (1) the President
   (2) the Constititution
   (3) Congress
   (4) amendments

6. Which of the following statements best gives the main idea of the passage?

   (1) The Constitution is the main law of the United States.
   (2) The only way that the Constitution can be changed is through an amendment.
   (3) The word *amendment* means "change."
   (4) The President cannot order an amendment.

Check your answers on page 79.

UNIT REVIEW

In this unit, you've worked on finding the main idea of a reading passage. The main idea of a passage is the main thing that a passage says. It's the main point that a passage makes.

In this unit, you've seen that some passages contain a main idea sentence. Sometimes, the main idea sentence is at the beginning of the passage. But sometimes the main idea sentence appears later in the passage. To understand the main idea, you have to think about the *entire* passage. You have to figure out what all the details in the passage add up to.

In the next unit, you'll take a closer look at the details of a passage. You'll look at how details are put together in the passage. You'll work on ways to find answers to questions about the details of a passage.

CLOSE-UP ON SCIENCE

In this unit, you read some passages about **cells**. The study of cells is part of the branch of science known as **biology**. Biology is the study of living things. **Biologists**—people who study biology—study plants and animals.

Biology is one branch of science. But biology itself is made up of many branches. The study of plant life is called **botany**. The study of animal life is called **zoology**. **Microbiology** is the study of living things that can only be seen through a microscope. **Structural biology** is the study of how organisms are put together. **Biochemistry** is the study of the chemistry of living things. **Ecology** is the study of how plants and animals live together in the environment.

Try It: Close-up on Science

The following words are from science passages in this unit. Fill in the blanks in the sentences with the correct words from the list.

antibodies   cancer   cells   chloroplasts   genes

1. All living things are made of _____ .

2. _____ attack germs that do not belong in the body.

3. _____ is a disease of the body's cells.

4. _____ allow plants to produce their own food.

5. _____ give a living thing its special features.

Check your answers on page 79.

CLOSE-UP ON SOCIAL STUDIES

In this unit, you read some passages about **government**. You read about the branches of the U.S. government. You read about how laws are passed.

The study of government comes under the branch of social studies known as **political science**. All societies have rules. The rules are usually written as laws. Governments usually make the laws and enforce them. **Political scientists** study different governments and their laws. They study the different ways that societies have organized.

A good way to understand how government works is to read the newspaper. Newspapers are filled with stories about government, laws, and political leaders. You can use newspaper stories to increase your understanding of how government works.

Try It: Close-up on Social Studies

The following words are from social studies passages in this unit. Fill in the blanks in the following sentences with the correct words from the list.

| amendment | Constitution | Congress | judicial |
| executive | legislative | checks and balances | |

1. Congress is the _____ branch of the U.S. government.

2. The _____ branch of the U.S. government includes the President.

3. The _____ branch of the U.S. government is headed by the Supreme Court.

4. The system of _____ forces the branches of government to work together.

5. Together, the Senate and House of Representatives make up _____ .

6. The _____ is the main law of the United States.

7. The only way that the Constitution can be changed is through an _____ .

Check your answers on page 80.

CLOSE-UP ON LITERATURE

In this unit, you read some passages of nonfiction. Nonfiction is writing about something that really happened or that is known to be true. The writer may try only to report the facts, or may include opinions and descriptive details about them.

There are different kinds of nonfiction literature, and this unit includes several of them. Knowing about the different types and which one you are reading can help you understand more of what you read. A **biography** is the story of someone's life. When someone writes the story of his or her own life, that writing is called **autobiography**. This unit includes biography, autobiography, and a written account of someone talking about her life. Knowing what you are reading helps you to understand the writer's point of view.

Articles and **essays** are other kinds of nonfiction. In them, an author may discuss a particular subject. An article may be serious or funny, formal or relaxed, long or short. Other kinds of nonfiction literature include **diaries** (an account of just a part of someone's life) and **travelogues**. A travelogue is an account of a journey. Some writing may fit into more than one of these categories: a book could be both biography and travelogue, for example.

Try It: Close-up Literature

The following words are from the passage above. Fill in the blanks in the sentences with the correct words from the list.

article   autobiography   biography   nonfiction   travelogue

1. An author is writing a book about someone who died many years ago. That kind of book is called _____ .

2. A book that describes events that actually happened is _____ .

3. A _____ is a description of someone's experiences while on a trip.

4. A famous person might write a(n) _____ to talk about his or her life.

5. A short history of a town could be called an essay or a(n) _____.

Check your answers on page 80.

ANSWERS AND EXPLANATIONS

Try It: What Is the Main Idea?

1. The topic of the passage is the **branches of the national government**. From scanning, you could probably tell that the passage is about the branches of government. The details in the passage tell you about the three branches of government.

2. The main idea of the passage is that **the national government of the United States is divided into three branches**. The main idea is stated in the first sentence of the passage. The details of the passage tell you something about each branch of the government.

3. The topic of the passage is **"magic bullets."** The words *magic bullets* appear a number of times in the passage. The details of the passage tell you about "magic bullets."

4. The main idea of the passage is that **"magic bullets" are a new way to fight disease**. The main idea is stated in the first sentence of the passage. The details tell you what "magic bullets" are and how they can be used to fight disease.

5. The topic of the passage is **cancer**. The word *cancer* appears often in the passage. The details of the passage tell you about cancer cells and cancer genes.

6. The main idea of the passage is that **cancer is a disease of the body's cells**. The main idea is stated in the first sentence of the passage. The details tell you what cancer is and how it might start.

Try It: Digging for the Main Idea

1. The topic of the passage is **Congress**. The details of the passage tell you about the two bodies of Congress.

2. **(2)** The main idea is that Congress is divided into two bodies, the Senate and the House of Representatives. The details of the passage tell you about the two bodies of Congress.

3. The topic of the passage is **plant cells and animal cells.** The words *plant cells* and *animal cells* appear throughout the passage. The details of the passage tell you about plant cells and animal cells.

4. **(3)** The beginning of the passage tells you that plant and animal cells have a lot in common. But most of the passage tells you about the differences between plant and animal cells.

Try It: Answering Main Idea Questions

1. **(3)** The topic of the passage is a voting procedure. The other answer choices are only details. From reading the passage, you can tell that most of the passage gives details of the voting system.

2. **(2)** The main idea is that because of a peculiar voting system, it was all too easy for members of the House of Representatives to sit on the fence. The other answer choices are details that support that main idea.

3. **(3)** The topic of the passage is cosmetic testing. If you scan the passage, you see both words repeated many times. The other answer choices are only details.

4. **(3)** The main idea is supported by the details of the passage. The other answer choices only give details that support the main idea.

5. **(2)** The Constitution is the topic of the passage. If you scan the passage, you will see "Constitution" repeated many times. The other answer choices are details about the Constitution.

6. **(2)** The passage tells you the steps needed to change the Constitution. Answer choice 1, the first sentence of the passage, does *not* give the main idea of the passage. Answer choices 3 and 4 are details that add to the main idea, but they do not give the main idea.

Try It: Close-up on Science

1. All living things are made of **cells**. This information is given in the passage on page 66.

2. **Antibodies** attack germs that do not belong in the body. This information is given in the passage on page 67.

3. **Cancer** is a disease of the body's cells. This information is given in the passage on page 68.

4. **Chloroplasts** allow plants to produce their own food. This information is given in the passage on page 70.

5. **Genes** give a living thing its special features. This information is given in the passage on page 71.

Try It: Close-up on Social Studies

1. Congress is the **legislative** branch of the U.S. government. This information is given in the passage on page 67.

2. The **executive** branch of the U.S. government includes the President. This information is given in the passage on page 67.

3. The **judicial** branch of the U.S. government is headed by the Supreme Court. This information is given in the passage on page 67.

4. The system of **checks and balances** forces the branches of government to work together. This information is given in the passage on pages 68 and 69.

5. Together, the Senate and House of Representatives make up **Congress**. This information is given in the passage on page 70.

6. The **Constitution** is the main law of the United States. This information is given in the passage on page 74.

7. The only way that the Constitution can be changed is through an **amendment**. This information is given in the passage on page 74.

Try It: Close-up on Literature

1. An author is writing a book about someone who died many years ago. That kind of book is called **biography**.

2. A book that describes events that actually happened is **nonfiction**.

3. A **travelogue** is a description of someone's experiences while on a trip.

4. A famous person might write an **autobiography** to talk about his or her life.

5. A short history of a town could be called an essay or an **article**.

UNIT 5: FINDING DETAILS

In the last unit, you looked at finding the main idea of a reading passage. Finding the main idea is a basic reading skill. Reading tests often ask a lot of main idea questions.

In this unit, you'll work on another basic reading skill. You'll work on finding details in a reading passage. Reading tests ask questions about the details of a passage. If you can find the details, you can answer the questions easily. In this unit, you'll look at strategies for answering questions about the details that are given in a passage.

WHAT ARE DETAILS?

Everything that you read is made up of details. A detail is a piece of information. It's a piece of information that helps you to understand a passage. Usually, a detail is an answer to one of these questions:

- **Who?**
- **What?**
- **When?**
- **Where?**
- **Why?**
- **How?**

These six questions are often called "the 5 W's plus H." The answers to these six questions are usually the most important details of a passage.

A good way to understand "the 5 W's plus H" is to look at a newspaper story. The beginning of a news story usually contains the most important details. It usually answers "the 5 W's plus H" questions. For example, look at this story:

Two men were injured last night near Exit 16 on Highway 35 when their car skidded off the road and crashed into a tree.

Police identified the two men as Lowell T. Lovett and Randolph Hearn, both from Harrison, New York. Both men are reported in satisfactory condition at Valley General Hospital.

Police say that the car, which was driven by Lovett, skidded when it hit an oil slick on the road.

This is a pretty short news story. It's short, but it is filled with details. The details answer questions like these:

Who is the story about?

The story is about two men named Lowell T. Lovett and Randolph Hearn.

What happened to the two men?

They were injured.

When were they injured?

They were injured last night.

Where were they injured?

They were injured near Exit 16 on Highway 35.

How were they injured?

They were injured when their car skidded off the road and crashed into a tree.

Why did the car skid off the road?

Police say that the car skidded off the road when it hit an oil slick.

These are the most important questions about the story. These are the most important details of the story. But the story contains other details, too. The details answer these questions:

Who identified the two men?

Where are the two men from?

Where are the two men now?

What is their condition?

Who was driving the car when it crashed?

All of these questions are questions about the story's details. The details are given in the story. You could answer these questions just by looking back at the story and getting the right details from it.

Try It: What Are Details?

Read this story and then answer the questions about it.

It was Saturday afternoon. The little boy, Jody, came out of the house. He was eating a thick piece of buttered bread. He saw Billy Buck, the ranch hand, working on the last of the haystack. Jody tramped down scuffing his shoes in a way he had been told was harmful to good shoe-leather.

A flock of white pigeons flew out of the black cypress tree as Jody passed. The flock circled the tree and landed again. A half-grown cat leaped from the porch. It galloped on stiff legs across the road, whirled and galloped back again. Jody picked up a stone to help the game along. But he was too late, for the cat was under the porch before he could throw the stone. He threw the stone into the cypress tree and started the white pigeons on another whirling flight.

1. Who is this story about?

2. What was this person eating?

3. When does the story happen?

4. Where had Jody been?

5. Why did Jody pick up a stone?

6. How did Jody alarm the pigeons?

7. Who is Billy Buck?

8. What was Billy Buck doing?

Check your answers on page 100.

LOOKING AT HOW DETAILS FIT TOGETHER

The first step in understanding the details of a story is knowing what the details are. The second step is recognizing how they fit together.

You know that a reading passage is made up of details. Each detail adds a piece of information to the story. But the details usually aren't separate from one another. They usually fit together in some way. They are usually **organized** in some way.

Think back to Unit 2 of this book. In Unit 2, you looked at how ideas in a passage are organized. You worked on using this information to keep track of ideas as you read.

What are the ways in which details can be organized in a passage? Details can be organized in a number of ways. The way in which they are organized depends on the kinds of details that are in a passage. For example, look at these two sentences:

First, the car skidded across the highway. Then, it crashed into a tree.

The sentences tell you two things that happened. How are the two details put together? How are they organized?

The two details are put in **time order**. They are organized to show which one happened first. The first thing that happened was that the car skidded across the road. The second thing that happened was that it crashed into a tree.

Time order is one basic way that details are organized. Time order shows the order in which things occur. How can you tell when things are put in a time order? Take another look at the two sentences:

First, the car skidded across the highway. **Then**, it crashed into a tree.

The sentences contain key words. These words tell you how the details are organized. The words *first* and *then* tell you that the details are in a time order. Here are some other words that are often used to show a time order:

before   after   later
next   afterward   earlier

Time order is one way in which details can be put together. Here is another way:

The car skidded across the road **because** it hit an oil slick.

This sentence gives you two details. The car skidded across the road. It hit an oil slick. How are the two details put together? Again, there is a key word that shows how the details are organized. The key word is *because*. The word *because* shows that one thing **caused** another to happen.

Details are often organized to show that one thing caused another thing to happen. *Because* is a key word that shows cause. Here are some other key words that can show cause:

reason	therefore	as a result
thus	consequently	

Time order and cause are two basic ways that details are organized. Here are some other ways:

Comparison: Sometimes, things are compared in a passage. The passage gives details about their similarities and differences. For example, look at this passage:

For a year she had made her living playing the violin at the train station. She played without thinking much about her music. She spent more time watching the people. On one hand, there were those people who lingered to listen. They usually smiled at her and sometimes even made a nice remark about her playing. Sometimes they stayed for one or two songs. On the other hand, not everyone was a music-lover. There were people who rushed by, as though there were no time in the world for music. Often, these people didn't look at her, but when they did, it was with a frown. Some people dropped money into her open case. However, others dropped in used tickets or other pieces of trash.

In this passage, two things are being compared. The reactions of two kinds of people to music are being compared. In the passage, the words *On one hand*, *on the other hand*, *those*, *these*, *some*, and *others* are clues that things are being compared and contrasted. These words, along with the words *still*, *nevertheless*, and *yet*, are often used in comparisons.

Classification: Sometimes, details are organized in groups. The passage shows which things belong in which groups. Details that are organized in groups are classified. For example, look at this passage:

There are several branches of social studies. One of the branches is called "behavioral science." Behavioral science is the study of human behavior. Behavioral science itself is made up of several branches. Psychology is one branch of behavioral science. Psychology is the study of the human mind. Another branch of behavioral science is sociology. Sociology is the study of how humans act in groups. A third branch of behavioral science is cultural anthropology. This is the study of the values and beliefs that make up a culture.

This passage is about behavioral science. It tells you the branches that make up behavioral science. From the passage you can tell that psychology, sociology, and cultural anthropology are all branches of behavioral science. The passage explains that they belong in the behavioral science group.

There are four basic ways that details are organized in a passage. The four basic ways are time order, cause, comparison, and classification. Knowing these four basic ways can help you to answer a lot of questions about the details of a reading passage.

Try It: Looking at How Details Fit Together

Read the next four passages. Then answer the questions that follow. Each passage is organized in one of the four basic ways that you just read about.

Passage #1

"There are three kinds of people in this world," said Uncle Van, and then he paused to make sure my sister and I were paying attention. "Well, Uncle," said Carrie impatiently, "what are they?"

"Oh, you'd like to hear about them?" said Uncle Van, pretending to be surprised. "Well, the first kind of people are the ones who get out of bed early every morning, just as I do. They're the people who get things done in this world.

"The second kind of people are those who get up late. They're the lazy ones. They sleep all day, and they seldom accomplish much of anything."

Then Uncle Van stared hard at both of us and continued. "The third kind are people who sit around listening to stories. They can get up early or late. Whenever they get up, they're happy to listen to someone else tell them things so they don't have to learn for themselves."

Passage #2

Do blind people have dreams? If so, what are their dreams like? Scientists say that blind people do dream. A person who is born blind has one kind of dream. On the other hand, a person who loses his sight later in life has another kind of dream. A person who is born blind does not see anything in his dreams. His dreams tell a story based on sounds and feelings. A person who goes blind later in life, however, can see his dreams. His brain can remember how the world looks. It can even make new pictures based on things the person once saw. Do dreams without pictures seem less real? No, all dreams tell a story that seems real. A dream based on sounds and feelings seems just as real.

Passage #3

Learning to relax could add years to your life. Studies show that aggressive, impatient people are more likely to get heart disease. This is because stress can cause dangerous chemicals to be released into a person's blood. Over many years, these chemicals can result in high blood pressure and hardening of the arteries. Stress can also cause the body to become weak and make it more prone to disease. Stress can even make an existing disease worse. In addition, stress can make a person feel depressed and unable to cope with daily life. When this happens, a person is more likely to turn to smoking, drugs, or alcohol.

Passage #4

I was never kinder to the old man than during the whole week before I killed him. And every night, about midnight, I turned the latch of his door and opened it—oh, so gently! And then, when I had made an opening sufficient for my head, I put in a dark lantern, all closed, closed, so that no light shone out, and then I thrust in my head. Oh, you would have laughed to see how cunningly I thrust it in! I moved it slowly—very, very slowly, so that I might not disturb the old man's sleep. It took me an hour to place my whole head within the opening so far that I could see him as he lay upon his bed.

1. In which passage are the details organized in time order?

    (1) Passage #1
    (2) Passage #2
    (3) Passage #3
    (4) Passage #4

2. In which passage are the details organized to show causes?

    (1) Passage #1
    (2) Passage #2
    (3) Passage #3
    (4) Passage #4

3. In which passage are the details organized to show comparisons?

    (1) Passage #1
    (2) Passage #2
    (3) Passage #3
    (4) Passage #4

4. In which passage are the details organized according to classification?

    (1) Passage #1
    (2) Passage #2
    (3) Passage #3
    (4) Passage #4

Check your answers on page 100.

WORKING WITH LONGER PASSAGES

So far, you've worked on looking at how short passages are put together. The details of each passage were organized in one particular way.

Now, take a look at this longer passage. How are the details of this passage organized?

Photosynthesis is a very important process. It is the process in which green plants make food and release oxygen into the air. All life on earth depends on photosynthesis.

The steps involved in photosynthesis are very simple. First, the green plant takes in two things. It takes in water through its roots. It takes in carbon dioxide from the air through small openings in its leaves. The water makes its way up through the plant to the leaves. The water and carbon dioxide come together in the cells of the plant's leaves.

The next step in photosynthesis involves sunlight. Sunlight hits the leaves. The plant's cells get energy from the sunlight. They then use the energy to combine the water and carbon dioxide together. The atoms of water and carbon dioxide combine to form glucose, which is a sugar. Oxygen atoms that are left over from the process are released back into the air. The plant uses some of the glucose for energy, and it stores the rest.

Why is it that only green plants can carry out the process of photosynthesis? The answer to this question also is simple. Only green plants can carry out photosynthesis because only green plants have chlorophyll. Chlorophyll is a substance that is located in the cells of the leaves of green plants. Chlorophyll is located in the part of the cell called the chloroplast. Photosynthesis cannot take place without chlorophyll.

This passage is longer than the ones that you've seen so far in this unit. This passage contains more details. The details of the passage are organized, but they are organized in a few ways. The first paragraph tells you what photosynthesis is. The details of the first paragraph are organized to give you a definition of photosynthesis. The second and third paragraphs tell you the steps involved in photosynthesis. The details are organized to show the order of the steps. The last paragraph explains why only green plants can carry out photosynthesis. The details are organized to explain the reason.

When you read a longer passage, you should keep track of how the details of the passage are organized. In Unit 2 of this book, you looked at keeping track of ideas as you read. In that unit, you worked on taking notes to keep track of things. Taking notes can help you to keep track of how details are organized in longer passages. For example, look at the notes on the next page on the passage about photosynthesis.

1. Introduction—tells what photosynthesis is

Photosynthesis is a very important process. It is the process in which green plants make food and release oxygen into the air. All life on earth depends on photosynthesis.

2. Gives the order of the steps in photosynthesis

The steps involved in photosynthesis are very simple. First, the green plant takes in two things. It takes in water through its roots. It takes in carbon dioxide from the air through small openings in its leaves. The water makes its way up through the plant to the leaves. The water and carbon dioxide come together in the cells of the plant's leaves.

The next step in photosynthesis involves sunlight. Sunlight hits the leaves. The plant's cells get energy from the sunlight. They then use the energy to combine the water and carbon dioxide together. The atoms of water and carbon dioxide combine to form glucose, which is a sugar. Oxygen atoms that are left over from the process are released back into the air. The plant uses some of the glucose for energy, and it stores the rest.

3. Explains why only green plants can carry out photosynthesis

Why is it that only green plants can carry out the process of photosynthesis? The answer to this question also is simple. Only green plants can carry out photosynthesis because only green plants have chlorophyll. Chlorophyll is a substance that is located in the cells of the leaves of green plants. Chlorophyll is located in the part of the cell called the chloroplast. Photosynthesis cannot take place without chlorophyll.

Taking notes on how the details of a passage are organized can be very helpful. It can help you to answer questions about the details of a passage. For example, look at this question:

According to the passage, what happens after a green plant gets energy from sunlight?

(1) It uses the energy to take in water through its roots.
(2) It uses the energy to take in carbon dioxide through small openings in its leaves.
(3) It uses the energy to combine water and carbon dioxide to form glucose.

The question asks you about the steps in photosynthesis. It asks you to tell what the next step is after the green plant gets energy from sunlight. Look at the notes on the passage. Where would you find the details to answer this question?

You'd find the details in the second part of the passage. The second part gives the order of the steps in photosynthesis. Using the notes, you can tell that the answer to the question is in either the second or third paragraph. You don't have to reread the whole passage to find the answer to the question. You can find the answer just by looking at the second and third paragraphs. The beginning of the third paragraph contains the answer to the question. The plant uses the energy from sunlight to combine water and carbon dioxide together. Answer choice 3 is the correct answer.

Try It: Working with Longer Passages

Here are two more passages. As you read each passage, look at how the details are organized. Write down notes about how the details are organized. Then use your notes to find the answers to the questions that follow the passage.

Everything is made up of atoms. It's hard to imagine how small an atom is. Atoms are so small that they can't be seen even with the strongest microscope. Atoms themselves are made up of even smaller particles called protons, neutrons, and electrons.

Fewer than 110 different kinds of atoms are known to exist. These different kinds of atoms are called elements. Some common elements are oxygen, hydrogen, carbon, and iron. Everything is made up of a combination of elements. A compound is a combination of two or more elements. For example, water is a compound. It is made up of two elements: hydrogen and oxygen. Salt is another common compound. Salt is made up of the elements sodium and chlorine. Sugar is another common compound. It is made up of the elements carbon, oxygen, and hydrogen.

What makes one kind of atom different from another kind of atom? All atoms are made up of protons, neutrons, and electrons. The difference between kinds of atoms lies in the *number* of protons, neutrons, and electrons that the atoms contain. For example, an atom of oxygen is made up of 8 protons, 8 neutrons, and 8 electrons. But an atom of carbon is made up of 6 protons, 6 neutrons, and 6 electrons. Carbon and oxygen atoms are made up of the same three particles. But the atoms are different because of the number of particles they contain.

1. Which of the following is an example of an element?

    (1) carbon
    (2) salt
    (3) sugar

2. Which of the following is an example of a compound?

    (1) chlorine
    (2) water
    (3) hydrogen

3. According to the passage, one kind of atom is different from another kind of atom because of

    (1) the different kinds of particles that the atoms contain
    (2) the different combinations of particles that the atoms contain
    (3) the different numbers of particles that the atoms contain

There were on the planet where the little prince lived—as on all planets—good plants and bad plants. In consequence, there were good seeds from good plants, and bad seeds from bad plants. But seeds are invisible. They sleep deep in the heart of the earth's darkness. Then some one among them is seized with the desire to awaken. This little seed will stretch itself. It will begin—timidly at first—to push a charming little sprig upward toward the sun. If it is only a radish sprout or the sprig of a rose-bush, one would let it grow wherever it might wish. But when it is a bad plant, one must destroy it as soon as possible, the very first instant that one recognizes it.

Now there were some terrible seeds on the planet that was the home of the little prince. These were the seeds of the baobab. The soil of that planet was infested with them. A baobab is something you will never, never be able to get rid of if you attend to it too late. It spreads over the entire planet. It bores clear through it with its roots. And if the planet is too small, and the baobabs are too many, they split it in pieces. . . .

"It is a question of discipline," the little prince said to me later on. "You must see to it that you regularly pull up all the baobabs. You must do it at the very first moment when they can be distinguished from the rosebushes which they resemble so closely in their earliest youth."

4. According to the passage, when must one destroy bad plants?

    (1) while they are still seeds
    (2) while they are sprigs
    (3) as soon as they can be recognized

5. What plant does the little prince think that baobabs resemble?

   (1) good plants
   (2) rosebushes
   (3) radishes

6. According to the passage, which of the following describes baobabs?

   (1) They are invisible.
   (2) They can be allowed to grow anywhere.
   (3) They can split a small planet into many pieces.

Check your answers on page 101.

ANSWERING QUESTIONS ABOUT DETAILS

The GED Tests include a lot of questions about details. If you know something about the kinds of questions that are asked, you'll find it easier to answer the questions.

How can you tell when a question is asking about the details of a passage? Look at this question from the last exercise:

According to the passage, when must one destroy bad plants?

The question begins with the words *according to the passage*. A phrase like this tells you that the answer to the question is stated in the passage. It is a detail from the passage.

Here are some other words and phrases that are used in details questions:

The passage states that . . .

Which of the following is mentioned in the passage . . .

When you are answering a details question, the first thing to do is to look at the question carefully. What is the question asking? Look for key words that can help you to figure out what the question is asking.

Read the next passage. As you read, take notes on how the passage is organized. Then look at the questions that follow it.

Sociology is the study of how humans act in groups. Sociologists study the way people act in different kinds of groups. The largest kind of group that sociologists study is a society. For example, a sociologist may study American society or Chinese society. A society is made up of smaller groups. Some of the smaller groups are called primary groups. Some are called secondary groups.

A primary group is made up of people who have close relationships. The relationships often last a lifetime. One example of a primary group is a family. Another example is a peer group. A peer group is a group of friends.

A secondary group is different from a primary group. People in primary groups have close relationships, but people in secondary groups usually do not. Also, secondary group relationships usually don't last as long as primary group relationships. One example of a secondary group is a group of workers in a factory. The workers belong to the same group, but they don't have close relationships.

Now, look at this question about the passage:

The passage states that one difference between primary and secondary groups is that relationships in a primary group are

(1) close
(2) short
(3) happy

This question asks you to identify a *difference* between primary and secondary groups. As you read the passage, you probably noted something about the third paragraph. You probably noted that the third paragraph compares primary and secondary groups. You can guess that you'll find the answer to this question in the third paragraph. The third paragraph tells you that relationships in primary groups are close, but they are not close in secondary groups. Answer choice 1 is correct.

Here is another kind of details question that you should know about:

Which of the following is NOT mentioned in the passage about relationships among people in a primary group?

(1) Relationships in a primary group are close.
(2) Relationships in a primary group often last a lifetime.
(3) Relationships in a primary group are happy.

Take a close look at the question stem. What is it asking you? It is asking you to choose the answer that is NOT mentioned as a detail in the passage.

Reading tests often contain this kind of details question. The GED Tests have questions like this one. To answer a question like this, you have to choose the detail that is not mentioned in the passage. The best way to answer a question like this is to go back to the passage. Look for each detail that is listed in the answer choices. The detail that you can't find is the correct answer to the question.

Take another look at the question. The question asks about relationships in primary groups. From your notes, you can guess that the details about this can be found in the second paragraph. The second paragraph says that primary group relationships are close. It says that they often last a lifetime. However, it does *not* say that primary group relationships are happy. Answer choice 3 is *not* given as a detail in the passage. Therefore, answer choice 3 is the correct answer to this question.

When you are answering a question about the details of a passage, remember these things:

1. Read the question carefully. Look for key words that can help you to understand what the question is asking.

2. Try to use the key words with your notes about the passage. This can help you to find the answer to a details question quickly.

3. Double-check the question stem. Sometimes, a question asks you to choose a detail that is *not* given in the passage.

Try It: Answering Questions About Details

Read the passage, and take notes on how the details of the passage are organized. Then try to use the notes to find the answers to the questions.

At one time or another, almost everyone has thrown away a rusty tool or watched a car body slowly rust away. Rust seems to be a disease that eats away metal.

But rust isn't a disease—it's a result of a chemical reaction. Rust is caused when a material containing iron is left in damp air. Damp air contains water vapor. Water vapor is made up of hydrogen and oxygen atoms. When iron is left in damp air, oxygen atoms from water vapor bond—or come together—with iron atoms. They bond to form a compound called iron oxide, or rust.

Here are some things you can do to prevent rust from ruining metal. The first thing is to try to keep anything made with iron in a dry place. You can also protect iron from rusting by coating the iron with a material that resists rusting. Oil and spray-on plastic can help to stop rust from forming.

1. According to the passage, rust is a

   (1) disease
   (2) result of a chemical reaction
   (3) form of water vapor
   (4) form of hydrogen

2. The passage states that rust forms when oxygen atoms from water vapor bond with

   (1) iron atoms
   (2) hydrogen atoms
   (3) iron oxide
   (4) oil or spray-on plastic

3. The passage mentions all of the following about rust EXCEPT:

   (1) Rust is also known as iron oxide.
   (2) Rust is caused when a material containing iron is left in damp air.
   (3) Rust is the result of a chemical reaction.
   (4) Rust cannot be prevented.

Check your answers on page 101.

UNIT REVIEW

In this unit, you've taken a close look at finding details as you read. Details are the pieces of information that make up a passage. Details are usually answers to these questions: *Who? What? When? Where? Why? How?* You've also looked at how details fit together in a passage. You've worked on using your knowledge of how details are organized to answer questions about details.

In the second section of this book, you've worked on answering questions about information that is stated in a passage. In the next section, you'll be doing something else. You'll be working on figuring out information that is *not* stated in a passage.

CLOSE-UP ON SCIENCE

In this unit, you read some passages about photosynthesis, atoms, and rust. All of these passages have one thing in common.

They all relate to the branch of science called **chemistry**. Chemistry deals with what things are made of and how things change. What are the elements that make up water? What happens to water when it freezes? What happens to water when it evaporates? How do green plants produce food? What causes rust? The answers to these questions and other questions like these are a part of chemistry.

The passage about atoms in this unit contains some basic information about chemistry. The passage tells you something about **atomic theory**—the theory of how an atom works. The theory is based on all the evidence that chemists have about atoms. It's based on evidence because no one has really seen an atom work. Atoms are too small to be seen even with the most powerful microscopes.

Try It: Close-up on Science

The following words are from science passages in this unit. Fill in the blanks in the sentences with the correct words from the list.

carbon dioxide	chlorophyll	compound	electrons
elements	glucose	neutrons	protons
photosynthesis			

1. Different kinds of atoms are called _____ .

2. A _____ is a combination of two or more elements.

3. Atoms are made up of _____ , _____ , and _____ .

4. _____ is the process in which green plants make food and release oxygen into the air.

5. To make food, a green plant takes in _____ through small openings in its leaves.

6. In photosynthesis, a green plant makes _____ , which is a kind of sugar.

7. Only green plants can carry out photosynthesis because only green plants contain _____ .

Check your answers on page 102.

CLOSE-UP ON SOCIAL STUDIES

In this unit, you read some passages about **behavioral science**. Behavioral science is the branch of social studies that deals with people. What makes a person act in a particular way? What makes a group act in a particular way? How did people act in the past? What kinds of societies existed in the past? The answers to questions like these involve the branches of behavioral science.

Behavioral science is an important branch of social studies. Behavioral scientists try to understand what people do and why they do it. They try to explain why people act and feel the way they do. They try to figure out how events and rules affect the way people think and act.

Try It: Close-up on Social Studies

The following words are from social studies passages in this unit. Fill in the blanks in the sentences with the correct words from the list.

cultural anthropology primary group psychology
secondary group   society   sociology

1. _____ is the study of the human mind.

2. _____ is the study of how humans behave in groups.

3. _____ is the study of the values and beliefs that make up a culture.

4. The largest kind of group that sociologists study is a _____.

5. A _____ is made up of people who have close relationships.

6. A _____ is made up of people whose relationships usually aren't close.

Check your answers on page 102.

CLOSE-UP ON LITERATURE

In this unit, you read some passages of **fiction**. Fiction is a made-up story, something that has been imagined by the writer. It differs from nonfiction, which describes something that really happened. This unit includes both **fantasy** and **realistic fiction**. Fantasy describes things that are completely make-believe. Realistic fiction, on the other hand, is true to life.

Fiction contains literary elements not usually found in nonfiction. The **plot** is the sequence of events in the story. The **characters** are the people who take part in the story. The **setting** is the time and place in which the events take place. All of these are made vivid by descriptive details, as you have seen in this unit. It helps to notice literary elements, such as plot, character, and setting, because they indicate what the story is about and how it works.

The author of fiction may use a **narrator**, someone who tells the story. Recognizing the narrator can help you understand both a stated and an implied main idea. When you read fiction, ask yourself, "Is the narrator taking part in the story? Or is the narrator an independent observer, describing the events from the outside?" Realizing who is telling the story helps to understand the narrator's point of view. The passages you have read in this unit represent different narrative points of view.

Try It: Close-up on Literature

The following words are from the passage above. Fill in the blanks in the sentences with the correct words from the list.

plot   narrator   setting   fantasy   characters

1. The _____ tells the story.

2. Science fiction is a kind of _____.

3. The _____ is the series of events in a story.

4. Details about the _____ tell you more about the people in a story.

5. The time and place of a story is called its _____.

Check your answers on page 102.

ANSWERS AND EXPLANATIONS

Try It: What Are Details?

1. This story is about Jody. It tells you what Jody did.

2. Jody was eating a thick piece of buttered bread. The answer to this question is in the third sentence of the story.

3. The story happens on a Saturday afternoon. The answer to this question is in the first sentence of the story.

4. Jody had been in the house. The answer to this question is in the second sentence of the story.

5. Jody picked up a stone to help the game along. The answer to this question is in the second paragraph.

6. Jody alarmed the pigeons by throwing the stone into the cypress tree. The answer to this question is in the last sentence.

7. Billy Buck is the ranch hand. The answer to this question is in the fourth sentence.

8. Billy Buck was working on the last of the haystack. The answer to this question is in the fourth sentence.

Try It: Looking at How Details Fit Together

1. (4) The details of the passage are organized to show the **order of the events** before the old man was killed. The words *before, then*, and *when* show that the details are organized in time order.

2. (3) The details of the passage tell you how stress can **cause** health problems. Such words as *because, cause*, and *result* show that the details are organized to show cause.

3. (2) In Passage #2, different kinds of dreams are **compared**. The phrase *on the other hand* and the word *however* are used to compare the different kinds of dreams.

4. (1) The passage tells you about three different kinds of people. It classifies people into categories. The categories are people who get things done, people who don't get things done, and people who learn everything from other people.

Try It: Working with Longer Passages

1. **(1)** Carbon is an example of an element. You can find this detail in the second paragraph. The second paragraph gives examples of elements and compounds.

2. **(2)** Water is an example of a compound. You can find this detail in the second paragraph. The second paragraph gives examples of elements and compounds.

3. **(3)** The passage says that one kind of atom is different from another kind of atom because of the different numbers of particles that the atoms contain. You can find this detail in the last paragraph. The last paragraph compares different kinds of atoms.

4. **(3)** According to the passage, one must destroy bad plants as soon as they can be recognized. You can find this detail in the first paragraph.

5. **(2)** The little prince thinks that baobabs resemble rosebushes. You can find this detail in the third paragraph. The third paragraph gives the little prince's opinions about baobabs.

6. **(3)** The passage says that baobabs can split small planets into pieces. You can find this detail in the second paragraph. The second paragraph describes the damage that baobabs can cause. The paragraph is organized by cause.

Try It: Answering Questions About Details

1. **(2)** The question asks you to tell what rust is. The second paragraph tells you that rust is the result of a chemical reaction.

2. **(1)** The question asks you to find a detail about how rust is formed. The second paragraph gives you these details. It says that oxygen atoms from water vapor bond—or come together—with iron atoms to form rust.

3. **(4)** The passage does NOT say that rust cannot be prevented. This question asks you to choose the detail that is *not* mentioned in the passage. The first three details are all mentioned in the second paragraph. However, the last detail is *not* mentioned. In fact, the third paragraph tells you how you can prevent rust.

Try It: Close-up on Science

1. Different kinds of atoms are called **elements**. This information is on page 91.

2. A **compound** is a combination of two or more elements. This information is on page 91.

3. Atoms are made up of **protons**, **neutrons**, and **electrons**. This information is on page 91.

4. **Photosynthesis** is the process in which green plants make food and release oxygen into the air. This information is on page 88.

5. To make food, a green plant takes in **carbon dioxide** through small openings in its leaves. This information is on page 89.

6. In photosynthesis, a green plant makes **glucose**, which is a kind of sugar. This information is on page 89.

7. Only green plants can carry out photosynthesis because only green plants contain **chlorophyll**. This information is on page 89.

Try It: Close-up on Social Studies

1. **Psychology** is the study of the human mind. This information is on page 86.

2. **Sociology** is the study of how humans behave in groups. This information is on page 86 and page 94.

3. **Cultural anthropology** is the study of the values and beliefs that make up a culture. This information is on page 86.

4. The largest kind of group that sociologists study is a **society**. This information is on page 94.

5. A **primary group** is made up of people who have close relationships. This information is on page 94.

6. A **secondary group** is made up of people whose relationships usually aren't close. This information is on page 94.

Try It: Close-up on Literature

1. The **narrator** tells the story.

2. Science fiction is a kind of **fantasy**.

3. The **plot** is the series of events in a story.

4. Details about the **characters** tell you more about the people in a story.

5. The time and place of a story is called its **setting**.

Interpreting What You Read

In the second section of this book, you worked on the basics of reading for information: finding the main idea of a passage and finding the details in a passage. You used the organization of details to answer questions about details. You answered questions about things that were stated in the passage.

In this section you will learn how to answer questions about things that are not mentioned in a passage—questions like many on the GED. Briefly, to answer such questions, you use your skill at finding details that are provided. Those details become the clues that point to the answers you need.

The units in this section, like those in the second section, end with Close-ups on science, social studies, and literature. They will help you expand your knowledge of those three subjects even further.

UNIT 6: FINDING THE UNSTATED MAIN IDEA

What is a main idea? You answered this question in Unit 4 of this book. In that unit, you worked on finding the main idea of a passage. The main idea is the main thing that the passage says about its topic.

Each passage in Unit 4 contained a statement that gave the main idea. But many passages don't have a main idea sentence. The main idea is *unstated*.

How do you find the main idea of a passage that doesn't have a stated main idea? Actually, it's not too hard. A main idea sentence gives you the main idea. But, when you read a passage, you don't always know which sentence gives the main idea. The main idea sentence can be anywhere in the passage. You have to *think* about which sentence states the main idea.

To find the unstated main idea, you also have to think. You have to answer some questions about the passage. What is the topic? What are the details? How are the details organized? Together, what do the details say about the topic? What is the main point that the author of the passage is trying to make? The answers to these questions will help you to find a main idea that isn't stated. In this unit, you'll work on strategies for finding an unstated main idea in a passage. You'll also work on ways to answer questions about main ideas that are not stated.

PUTTING THE MAIN IDEA TOGETHER

The main idea of a passage is made up of two parts. The first part is the topic. The second part is a statement about the topic.

The first step in putting a main idea together is to figure out the passage's topic. This is usually pretty easy to do. For example, look at this passage:

There are rich countries, and there are poor countries. Saudi Arabia is a rich country. It has one major natural resource: oil. Oil is a natural resource that is in very high demand around the world. Saudi Arabia is rich because of its natural resource. Bangladesh is a poor country. It has natural resources. But none of its natural resources are as valuable as oil. Bangladesh is poor because it doesn't have a valuable natural resource like oil.

What is the topic of this passage? You could probably figure out the topic just by scanning the passage. The words *natural resource* and *natural resources* appear several times in the passage. The topic of the passage is natural resources.

What is the main point that the passage makes about natural resources? To answer this question, you have to think about the passage's details. What does the passage say? Together, what point do the details make?

The passage tells you about two countries. One of the countries is rich. The other is poor. The passage says that Saudi Arabia is rich because of its natural resource. It also says that Bangladesh is poor because it doesn't have a valuable natural resource like oil. In other words, a country's wealth depends on its natural resources. This is the main idea of the passage.

Look at the passage again. You won't find this main idea stated in the passage. This passage does not contain a main idea sentence. But if you think about the passage's details, the main idea is clear.

There's no trick to figuring out the main idea of a passage. The way to figure out the main idea is to first find the passage's topic. Then think about what the details tell you about the topic.

Here's another passage. It has something in common with the passage that you just read. As you read the next passage, think about what the details are telling you about the topic.

The major natural resource of Saudi Arabia is oil. Saudi Arabia's economy is based on the production and sale of oil. One of the major natural resources of Iceland is its ocean waters, which are filled with fish. Fishing is the most important part of Iceland's economy. Coal is a plentiful natural resource in Poland. A big part of Poland's economy is based on producing and using coal.

This passage has the same topic as the first passage that you read. The topic is natural resources. But the main idea of this passage is a little different from the main idea of the first passage. What do the details of this passage tell you?

The passage tells you about three countries. It tells you the major natural resource of each country. It also tells you something about the economy of each country. It tells you that the main natural resource of each country is also a main part of the country's economy. This is the main idea of the passage. Again, the passage does not contain a sentence that states the main idea. But the main idea is clear if you think about what the details are saying.

Remember that a main idea is made up of two parts. The first part is the topic of the passage. The second part is a statement about the topic. The topic is usually easy to figure out. But, in most cases, you have to think about the main thing that the passage says about the topic. What do the details say? What do they have in common? What point is the passage trying to make? The answers to these questions add up to the main idea.

Try It: Putting the Main Idea Together

Here are two more passages. Read each passage. As you read, try to figure out the main idea. Then answer the questions that follow the passage.

Twenty years ago, Al McBean opened his first fast-food restaurant. It was a small storefront place in Cincinnati, Ohio. That first year, McBean made a profit of only $1,000.

But McBean didn't give up the business. He stuck with it. After a few years, his business grew. Today, Al McBean owns 564 McBean's Burgers fast-food restaurants. He has restaurants in all 50 states and in 17 countries around the world, including Japan and Thailand. The 564 places netted McBean a profit of more than $7 million last year. And, this year, McBean expects things to get better. With the addition of 46 more McBean's Burgers restaurants, McBean expects his profits to increase by 15% this year.

1. What is the topic of this passage?

2. What is the main idea of this passage?

Two summers ago, the town of Tuggle Beach was blessed with perfect weather. Every weekend from May to September was sunny and hot. People came to Tuggle Beach in record numbers. People who owned businesses in the resort town made a lot of money two summers ago.

But last summer was a different story. The weather was very cool all summer long. It seemed that every weekend was a rainy one in Tuggle Beach. The town's businesses suffered. In fact, 10% of the businesses in Tuggle Beach didn't survive last summer. They went out of business.

This summer, the business owners in Tuggle Beach have their fingers crossed. They know that another cold and rainy summer could be a disaster. On the other hand, a season of good weather could make them all happy again.

3. What is the topic of this passage?

4. What is the main idea of this passage?

Check your answers on page 114.

USING ORGANIZATION TO FIND THE MAIN IDEA

In Unit 5 of this book, you looked at how details are organized in a passage. You worked on using the organization to answer questions about the details.

You can also use the organization to find the main idea of a passage. A lot of times, the way that details are put together will tell you something about the main idea. For example, look at this passage:

Corky Hairston is a farmer. He raises hogs. Normally, he uses corn to feed his hogs. But, for the past six months, Corky has been feeding his hogs with bread.

Last year was a bad one for corn growers. The weather was very hot and dry. Corn didn't grow well in the hot, dry weather. As a result, last year's corn crop wasn't very big. The price of corn rose because of this. Corky Hairston felt that the price of corn was too high. He found that buying bread was cheaper than buying corn for his hogs. So, for the time being, Corky's hogs are eating bread.

This passage is about Corky Hairston and his hogs. What is the main idea of the passage? To answer this question, look at how the passage is organized. What do the details tell you?

The details are organized to show a cause. The passage tells why Corky Hairston is feeding bread to his hogs. From the organization, you can tell something about the main idea. You can tell that the main idea will give you the reason that Corky is feeding bread to his hogs. Corky Hairston is feeding bread to his hogs because the price of corn is too high. This is the main idea of the passage.

Here is another passage. As you read it, think about how the details are organized. See if the organization can help you to find the passage's main idea.

In the 1970's, Atlantic City was a quiet town. It was also a poor town. Its major industry, tourism, was nearly dead. No one was going to Atlantic City.

Atlantic City isn't quiet any longer. Now, the city is filled with tourists. Thousands and thousands of people pour into Atlantic City every day. The people come for one main reason: to gamble. In the late 1970's, New Jersey decided to legalize gambling in Atlantic City. Since then, casino owners have spent millions of dollars to rebuild Atlantic City.

The topic of this passage is Atlantic City. What does the passage tell you about the topic? How are the details of the passage organized?

The first part of the passage tells you one thing. It tells you what Atlantic City was like in the 1970's. The second part of the passage tells you something else. It tells you what Atlantic City is like now. The passage compares the old Atlantic City and the new one. The details are organized to show a comparison.

What does the organization tell you about the main idea? The main idea of the passage is that legalized gambling has changed Atlantic City. The details are organized to show how the city has changed. The organization can give you a good clue to figuring out the passage's main idea.

When you are looking for a main idea, the most important thing to do is to think. Find the passage's topic. Think about what the passage says about the topic. Look at how the details of the passage are organized. Sometimes, the organization can give you a good clue to the main idea.

Try It: Using Organization to Find the Main Idea

Here is another passage. Read the passage. As you read, look at how the passage's details are organized. See if you can use the organization to figure out the passage's main idea. Then answer the questions that follow the passage.

What do you think of when you think of a map? If you're like most people, you probably think of a road map. Most people have used road maps.

But there are other kinds of maps you could have thought of. A political map is one important kind of map. A political map shows the boundaries of states and countries. It also shows the location of major cities. Another kind of map is a physical map. A physical map shows the location of lakes and rivers. It also shows the elevation of the land. There are other kinds of maps called special purpose maps. These maps may show special things about an area. For example, a special purpose map may show how the land in a country is used. It may show how the population of a country is spread out.

1. What is the topic of this passage?

2. Look at the details in the second paragraph of the passage. What do they tell you about?

3. Which of the following statements best gives the passage's main idea?

   (1) Road maps are an important kind of map.
   (2) Some kinds of maps are special purpose maps.
   (3) There are many different kinds of maps.

Check your answers on page 115.

ANSWERING QUESTIONS ABOUT
AN UNSTATED MAIN IDEA

You read earlier that reading tests often ask questions about the main idea of a passage. Some of these questions are about main ideas that are stated in the passage. But some of the questions are about unstated main ideas. Usually, questions about unstated main ideas look something like this:

Which of the following statements best gives the passage's main idea?

(1) Road maps are an important kind of map.
(2) Some kinds of maps are special purpose maps.
(3) There are many different kinds of maps.

This question asks you to pick the statement that best gives the passage's main idea. In other words, you have to read each statement and pick out the one that gives the main idea.

The best way to answer a question like this is through the process of elimination. In this process, you think about each separate answer choice. You think about whether the statement really gives the main idea. Only one of the statements gives the main idea. The others don't.

To see how the process of elimination works, read the next passage. Then look at the question that follows it. Think about the answer choices to the question.

Australia is about the same size as the continental United States. About 15 million people live in Australia. Most of them live in one area, along Australia's southeastern coast. Most of Australia is covered by either desert or rain forest. Very few people live in these areas. However, the southeastern coast has a temperate climate. This means that the weather does not get too hot or too cold, and there is plenty of rain. Most of Australia's cities are located along the southeastern coast.

Which of the following statements best gives the passage's main idea?

(1) Australia is a lot like the United States.
(2) A temperate climate is a climate in which the weather does not get too hot or too cold, and there is plenty of rain.
(3) Most of Australia's people live along Australia's southeastern coast because of its temperate climate.
(4) Very few people live in Australia.

Try using the process of elimination to answer the question. First, think about the passage itself. What do you think the main idea of the passage is? The passage tells you about Australia's climate and population. It says that most of Australia's people live along the southeastern coast. It says that the southeastern coast has a temperate climate. You can guess that the correct answer to the question will mention both of these things.

Now, look at the answer choices. Look at choice 1. Does the passage really tell you that Australia is a lot like the United States? Is that the passage's main idea? The passage does say that Australia is about as big as the continental United States. But that's all it says about the United States. The passage doesn't say that the two countries are alike. Therefore, you can eliminate answer choice 1. You can tell that it is not the correct answer.

Look at answer choice 2. Answer choice 2 tells you what a temperate climate is. But it doesn't mention anything about Australia. It doesn't mention anything about Australia's population. Answer choice 2 doesn't give enough information to be the main idea. You can eliminate it.

Now, look at answer choice 3. Answer choice 3 tells you that most of Australia's people live along Australia's southeastern coast. It also tells you why they live there. They live there because of the temperate climate. This statement covers the most important points of the passage. You can guess that answer choice 3 best states the main idea.

But, to make sure, look at answer choice 4. It says that very few people live in Australia. Is this mentioned in the passage? No, it isn't. The passage tells you that about 15 million people live in Australia. You may not think that that is a lot of people. But the passage doesn't say whether or not it's a lot of people. You have to answer the question based on what the passage says, not on your own opinions. Therefore, you can eliminate answer choice 4. Answer choice 3 is the correct answer.

You have to be careful when you answer a question about an unstated main idea. You have to make sure that your answer is based on the information that's in the passage. Don't answer the questions based on your own opinions. Think about each answer choice. Eliminate the ones that don't give enough information. Eliminate the ones that are not based on the information in the passage. Through the process of elimination, you'll have a very good chance of finding the passage's main idea.

Try It: Answering Questions About an Unstated Main Idea

Here are two more passages. Read each passage. Then answer the questions that follow the passage. Try to use the process of elimination to answer the questions.

Eight years ago, Moe Howard was on top of the boxing world. He was a world champion. He earned more than $1 million each time he fought.

Today, Moe Howard drives a milk truck. He earns about $220 a week. The millions that he earned in boxing are gone. His lawyers, agents, and "friends" took most of his money. The federal and state governments took the rest. Moe Howard fought in 46 professional fights. All he has to show for it are a few scars and a few memories.

Moe doesn't like to blame anybody for his problem. He puts the blame on himself. But, deep down, Moe Howard feels hurt. He trusted people to watch out for him and his money. The people that Moe trusted took his money and ran.

1. Which of the following statements best gives the passage's main idea?

    (1) Moe Howard was a good boxer.
    (2) Moe Howard earned too much money from his fights.
    (3) Moe Howard earns $220 a week driving a milk truck.
    (4) Moe Howard lost his money because the people he trusted let him down.

About 70% of the earth's surface is covered by water. This means that 30% of the earth's surface is land. But a majority of the world's population lives on only 7% of the land on earth. This means that more than half of the world's people live on 2% of the earth's surface.

Why does most of the world's population live on so little of the land? The answer could be climate. A lot of the earth's surface does not have a temperate climate. The climate is either too hot, too cold, or too dry. But a temperate climate is a moderate climate. People find it easier to live in a temperate climate. Only a small percentage of the land on earth has a temperate climate.

2. Which of the following statements best gives the passage's main idea?

(1) A temperate climate is a moderate climate.
(2) Most of the world's people are concentrated in areas that have a temperate climate.
(3) Most of the earth's surface is covered by water.
(4) People should learn to live in areas that don't have a temperate climate.

Check your answers on page 115.

UNIT REVIEW

In this unit, you've worked on finding the main idea of a passage. You've focused on finding a main idea when it is not stated in the passage. You've seen that finding an unstated main idea is a lot like finding a stated main idea. You have to think about the passage. You have to look at how the details are put together. You have to figure out the main thing that the passage is saying about its topic.

You've also looked at a strategy for answering main idea questions. You've worked on using the process of elimination to answer main idea questions. In this process, you look at each answer choice to a question. You eliminate the choices that are not correct.

In the next unit, you'll continue to work on figuring out things that are not stated in a passage. In the next unit, you'll work on making inferences about the details of a passage.

CLOSE-UP ON SOCIAL STUDIES

In this unit, you read a few passages that have something in common. You read passages about natural resources, maps, climate, and population. All of these topics are part of the branch of social studies called **geography.**

Geography is the study of the earth and its life. There are several important branches of geography. **Physical geography** is the study of the earth's physical features. These include continents, oceans, rivers, and mountains. **Cultural geography** is the study of the world's people. Cultural geographers study population patterns. They look at where people live and try to figure out why they live there.

Geography is a very basic part of social studies. It is the part of social studies that deals with the relationship of people to their environment.

Try It: Close-up on Social Studies

The following words are from social studies passages in this unit. Fill in the blanks in the sentences with the correct words from the list.

climate   natural resource   physical   political   population

1. A country's main _____ is often a major part of its economy.

2. A _____ map shows the boundaries of states and countries.

3. A _____ map shows the location of lakes and rivers, as well as the elevation of the land.

4. Most of the world's _____ lives in areas that have a temperate _____ .

Check your answers on page 115.

ANSWERS AND EXPLANATIONS

Try It: Putting the Main Idea Together

1. The topic of this passage is Al McBean and his fast-food restaurants, McBean's Burgers. All of the passage's details tell you about Al McBean and his restaurants. As you scanned the passage, you probably saw the names *Al McBean* and *McBean's Burgers* a number of times.

2. The main idea of this passage is that Al McBean has made McBean's Burgers into a very successful business. The first part of the passage tells you how small the business was when it first opened. The second part of the passage tells you how big and successful the business is now.

3. The topic of this passage is the weather in Tuggle Beach. All three paragraphs of the passage tell you something about the weather in Tuggle Beach. As you scanned the passage, you probably saw the name *Tuggle Beach* several times.

4. The main idea of this passage is that summer weather is very important in Tuggle Beach. Together, the details show you why the weather is important. The first paragraph tells you that Tuggle Beach does well when the summer weather is good. The second paragraph tells you that Tuggle Beach is in trouble when the weather is bad.

Try It: Using Organization to Find the Main Idea

1. The topic of this passage is maps. The passage tells you about several different kinds of maps. As you scanned the passage, you probably saw the word *map* a number of times.

2. The details in the second paragraph tell you about different kinds of maps. They tell you what some kinds of maps are and what they show.

3. **(3)** The main idea of the passage is that there are many different kinds of maps. The first paragraph tells you that most people have used a road map. The second paragraph tells you that road maps are only one kind of map; there are other kinds. Some other kinds of maps are described in the second paragraph.

Try It: Answering Questions About an
Unstated Main Idea

1. **(4)** The main idea of the passage is that Moe Howard lost his money because the people he trusted let him down. Use the process of elimination to answer this question. Answer choice 1 doesn't mention anything about Moe Howard's problem with money. Answer choice 2 is not supported by the passage. Answer choice 3 is only one detail from the passage. It doesn't give the passage's main idea. The details of the passage tell you who Moe Howard is and why he lost his money. Answer choice 4 is the correct answer.

2. **(2)** The main idea of the passage is that most of the world's people are concentrated in areas that have a temperate climate. The details of the passage tell you where most people live and why they live there. Answer choices 1 and 3 are only details from the passage. They don't give the main idea. Answer choice 4 is a statement that is not supported by the passage's details.

Try It: Close-up on Social Studies

1. A country's main **natural resource** is often a major part of its economy. This information is given in the passage on page 104.

2. A **political** map shows the boundaries of states and countries. This information is given in the passage on page 109.

3. A **physical** map shows the location of lakes and rivers, as well as the elevation of the land. This information is given in the passage on page 109.

4. Most of the world's **population** lives in areas that have a temperate **climate**. This information is given on page 112.

UNIT 7: MAKING BASIC INFERENCES

In Unit 5 of this book, you worked on finding details in a passage. You learned a few things about details in that unit. You learned that all reading passages are made up of details. A detail is a piece of information. In Unit 5, you worked on finding details that are stated in a passage. Most of the time, all of the important details are given in a passage. But sometimes they're not. Sometimes, you have to figure out some missing details. Sometimes, you have to make inferences about details that aren't stated in a passage.

In this unit, you'll take a close look at making inferences about the details of a passage. You'll look at how to figure out details that aren't stated in a passage. And you'll work on strategies to answer the kinds of inference questions that often appear on reading tests.

WHAT IS AN INFERENCE?

You may not have realized it, but you've been making inferences throughout this book. In the last unit, you made inferences about the main idea of a passage. Even in the first section of this book, you were making inferences. In that section you read this passage. And you answered a question about it.

"Are your clothes as clean as they should be? If they aren't, try Tring! Tring will make your clothes look better in no time! Your whites will look whiter! Your colors will look brighter!"

"So, throw out your old detergents! Get Tring! Your clothes will look like a million dollars!"

What is Tring?

When you answered this question, you made an inference. How did you answer the question? You thought about the information in the passage. You thought about the details that are stated in the passage. You put the pieces of information together to figure out the answer. The passage doesn't state what Tring is. But the details give you enough clues so that you can figure out what it is. Tring is a detergent.

Making an inference is a basic thinking and reading skill. When you make an inference, you figure something out. You use the facts or evidence that you know to figure out something that you don't know. When you read, you figure out details that aren't stated by putting together the details that are stated.

Try It: What Is an Inference?

Here are two examples of commentary—writing about literature or the arts. Try to figure out what is being reviewed.

There are many new comedies this fall. One new show is about two brothers who live with their mother. Another prime time show is about two brothers who live with their mother. In a third show, on the Comedy Network, a man inherits a restaurant.

There are also many new police shows this season. One show has an overweight private eye. A very rich businessman solves crimes in another show. Four shows have women police officers.

1. What is being described and reviewed?

If voice, posture, and gesture are the building blocks of acting, then the actors and actresses who appeared in this summer's series all need to go back to drama kindergarten. I was sitting in the eighth row, but even from that choice seat, I missed countless words that were mumbled and movements that were lost. Thank goodness none of the plays called for a stage whisper! Are today's actors all so set on television careers that they feel no need to practice for anything but the closeup shot and the microphone?

2. What is being described and reviewed?

Check your answers on pages 128 and 129.

USING DETAILS TO MAKE INFERENCES

When you make an inference you need one thing. You need evidence. You need details that will help you to make the inference.

Usually, the details that you need are pretty easy to find. For example, look at the next passage. Then look at the inference questions about it.

In May of 1787, a convention was held in Philadelphia. The purpose of the convention was to provide a stronger national government for the United States. The delegates to the convention agreed that they needed a stronger national law. They needed to either change or replace the Articles of Confederation.

What were the Articles of Confederation?

How did the delegates to the convention feel about the Articles of Confederation?

The details of the passage don't give you a direct answer to either of these questions. But the details give you enough information to figure out the answer to both questions. The details give you enough evidence to make some inferences.

Think about the first question. What were the Articles of Confederation? The passage doesn't tell you. But read the last two sentences of the passage again. Can you figure out what the Articles of Confederation were?

The passage tells you that the delegates agreed that they needed a stronger national law. The passage says they needed to either change or replace the Articles of Confederation. Put these two details together. You can infer that the Articles of Confederation *were* the national law. You made this inference based on the information in the passage.

Now, think about the second question. How did the delegates feel about the Articles of Confederation? The passage doesn't tell you directly how they felt. But it isn't hard to figure out with the information that is given. They agreed that they needed a stronger national law. They needed to either change or replace the Articles of Confederation. This means that they probably felt that the Articles of Confederation weren't strong enough. You can infer that the delegates felt that the Articles of Confederation weren't strong enough to be the national law.

Here is another passage. Read it, and then go on to the questions that follow it.

In 1803, the United States purchased the Louisiana Territory. Louisiana was a huge territory. It stretched west from the Mississippi River and covered what is now the midsection of the United States.

In many ways, the purchase of the Louisiana Territory was a matter of luck. France was almost at war with England. Napoleon did not think that he could protect Louisiana and its main port, New Orleans, from the strong English navy. Napoleon did not think that Louisiana was important enough to keep. He ordered his foreign minister, Charles Maurice de Tallyrand, to sell the territory. The United States bought the territory for about $15 million.

Who was Napoleon?

What country did the United States buy the Louisiana Territory from?

Again, the passage's details don't give you a direct answer to either question. But there's enough evidence in the passage to figure out the answers. Think about the first question. Can you figure out who Napoleon was? Look at the second paragraph of the passage. It tells you that France was almost at war with England. Then it says that Napoleon didn't think he could protect Louisiana from the English navy. In other words, he was worried that the English navy would attack the territory. England was nearly at war with France. The evidence leads you to figure out that Napoleon was French.

What else can you figure out about Napoleon? The passage tells you that he didn't think that Louisiana was important enough to keep. It also tells you that he ordered his foreign minister to sell the territory. From these details, you can infer that Napoleon was the leader of France.

Now, think about the second question. Once you've figured out who Napoleon was, the answer to the second question is easy. Napoleon was the leader of France. He ordered his foreign minister to sell the Louisiana Territory. The passage tells you that the United States bought the Louisiana Territory. You can infer that the United States bought the territory from France.

Making inferences is a basic thinking and reading skill. To make an inference, you need evidence. To make an inference when you read, you need to look for the evidence in the passage's details. Put the pieces of evidence together. Think about how the pieces fit together. Then see if the evidence can lead you to figure something out that isn't stated in the details.

Try It: Using Details to Make Inferences

Here are three more reading passages. Read each passage. Then go on to the inference questions that follow the passage. Use the evidence in the passage to answer the inference questions.

In the 1970s, Pacific Gas and Electric began building a nuclear power plant. The plant was at Diablo Canyon in California. Pacific Gas and Electric said the plant would allow it to provide cheap power to the area. But many people were against the plant. It was located only 2½ miles from Hosgri fault. A fault is a place where parts of the earth come together like pieces of a jigsaw puzzle. Earthquakes often occur at faults.

In 1975, the U.S. Geological Survey reported that a big earthquake could happen at Diablo Canyon. The agency said the earthquake could destroy the power plant. Pacific Gas and Electric disagreed. Then, in September 1981, the company said it had made a mistake. It admitted that parts of the plant could not survive an earthquake. These parts included the pipes that would carry dangerous nuclear fuel and radioactive wastes.

On November 19, 1981, the Nuclear Regulatory Commission shut down the Diablo Canyon plant. It said there had been a "serious breakdown" in safety at Diablo Canyon.

1. What is "Pacific Gas and Electric" the name of?

2. The passage says that many people were against the power plant at Diablo Canyon because it was located only 2½ miles from a fault. What do you think they were worried about?

3. Why did the Nuclear Regulatory Commission shut down the Diablo Canyon plant?

The American Civil War lasted for four long years. Hundreds of thousands of men were killed or wounded in the struggle. There were many reasons that the North ultimately won the war. One of the biggest reasons was its resources. The North had a larger army than the South. The North had more weapons and other supplies than the South.

At first, the South's strong military leadership was able to overcome these advantages. The first battle of Bull Run showed that the South had much better military leadership than the North. But, over time, the leadership advantage became less important. The superior resources of the North eventually led to General Robert E. Lee's surrender to the Union army at Appomattox Courthouse, Virginia, on April 9, 1865.

4. Who won the first battle of Bull Run?

5. When did the American Civil War end?

6. In what year did the American Civil War begin?

In April 1985, a great discovery was made when the old Cooke house in St. Louis was sold. A dozen sculptures and a trunk full of letters from Rupert Wright were found in the loft. The letters make it clear that Wright had created the sculptures during that period when he had vanished from the public eye.

Wright has long been admired as an oil painter of great imagination. However, there never before had been any hint that he had worked in any other medium. He had studied painting in Paris and become the center of a group of young artists. Then, in 1876, Wright dropped out of sight. He did not go out. He refused his friends' calls. If he painted, none of the results has ever been seen. Until last spring, the years from 1876 to 1885 were a total blank.

Then these mysterious sculptures appeared. They appear so modern—in line, texture, and composition—that it is hard to believe they were created in the nineteenth century. It is as though Wright spent those ten years in a time warp, studying under masters of the future. His "Wings" calls to mind Brancusi's "Bird in Flight." His sculpture of three life-sized figures makes one think of Henry Moore. Truly, this painter was a wonderful sculptor as well.

7. What does the author suggest that Wright was doing from 1876 to 1885?

8. Who were Brancusi and Moore, and what did they do?

Check your answers on pages 129 and 130.

ANSWERING INFERENCE QUESTIONS

When you answer an inference question, it's important to read the question stem carefully. That's because the stem will usually give you a good idea about the details that you need to make the inference. For example, read this passage and the question that follows it:

There are three basic types of rock: igneous rock, sedimentary rock, and metamorphic rock. Igneous rock is formed when liquid rock cools and hardens. If the magma hardens below the earth's surface, it is called intrusive rock. But if it escapes to the earth's surface as lava and hardens above the surface, it is called extrusive rock. Sedimentary rock is formed from dirt and sand. Metamorphic rock is rock that has had its chemical makeup or texture changed beneath the earth's surface.

From the information in the passage, you can infer that magma is

(1) sedimentary rock
(2) liquid rock
(3) one of the three basic types of rock

This question is asking you to infer what magma is. You need to find the details about magma. You can infer what magma is from the way that the details are put together. The second sentence is about the hardening of liquid rock. The third sentence is about the hardening of magma. You can infer that magma is liquid rock. Now, look at the answer choices to the question. Answer choice 2 is "liquid rock." Answer choice 2 is correct.

In the last unit, you worked on using the process of elimination to answer questions about an unstated main idea. You can use the process of elimination to check your answer to an inference question. For example, look at the inference question about magma. Look at answer choice 1. Does the passage give any evidence that magma is sedimentary rock? It says that sedimentary rock is formed from dirt and sand. The details about magma don't mention anything about sedimentary rock. You can eliminate answer choice 1.

Now, look at answer choice 3. Is there any evidence that magma is one of the three basic types of rock? The first sentence tells you that there are three basic types of rock: igneous rock, sedimentary rock, and metamorphic rock. It doesn't mention magma. There's no evidence that magma is one of the three basic types of rock. You can eliminate answer choice 3. That leaves answer choice 2, which is the correct answer.

Try It: Answering Inference Questions

Here are three more passages. Read them and answer the questions about them.

Last night the CBT Dance Troupe presented the first performance of "Sweet Land of Liberty." The piece dramatizes the civil rights movement of the 1960s, when blacks struggled to win the rights enjoyed by whites.

The dance began with two groups of performers. One group was dressed in white and wore stockings over their faces. The other group, clad in black, wore flat African-style masks. The black-clad dancers moved stealthily about the stage. The white-clothed dancers stood on pedestals placed around the stage.

In the next part of the dance, the movements of the black-clad dancers became bolder. Soon they were moving together in perfect time. The dancers on the pedestals began to jump around. Then they leaped down onto the stage, striking out at the dancers in black.

Suddenly all action onstage stopped when all the dancers fell to the floor. Then, slowly, a few of the dancers rose to their feet. In the dance's final moments, they removed their masks and mingled together.

"Sweet Land of Liberty" is a dance about strong emotions and intense conflict. It manages to be beautiful, graceful, and powerful.

1. Based on the information in the passage, who do the two groups of dancers represent?

   (1) Africans and Americans
   (2) men and women
   (3) blacks and whites
   (4) people who move stealthily and people who jump around

2. The ending of the dance implies that as a result of the civil rights movement

   (1) many people took up dancing
   (2) everyone involved in the struggle died
   (3) people no longer had to wear masks
   (4) some blacks and whites began to mingle together

3. You can infer that the author of this review thinks the new dance is

   (1) too dramatic
   (2) successful
   (3) bold
   (4) slow

The year 1933 was a year of great change in the United States. The first big change was in the presidency. On March 4, Franklin D. Roosevelt was sworn in as the nation's 32nd President. During the 1932 campaign, Roosevelt had promised that he would change the conservative policies of Herbert C. Hoover. Because of this promise, the nation elected Roosevelt over Hoover by a wide margin.

Americans waited to see what Roosevelt would do. They didn't have to wait for long. During the first 100 days of his presidency, Roosevelt carried out a number of bold steps. Each step was designed to pull America out of an economic depression. Not all of Roosevelt's plans worked. But many of them did. Many Americans began to feel more confident about the future.

Another big change occurred in 1933. The Twenty-first Amendment to the Constitution was ratified. The amendment did away with the nation's prohibition law. For the first time since 1920, Americans were able to drink liquor legally.

4. Based on the information in the passage, which of the following statements can you infer about America in 1933?

   (1) America was a very conservative country.
   (2) America was in an economic depression.
   (3) America did not support Franklin D. Roosevelt.
   (4) America was not a safe country to live in.

5. The passage implied that Franklin D. Roosevelt's steps during the first 100 days of his presidency were NOT

   (1) successful   (3) new
   (2) well-liked   (4) conservative

6. From the information in the passage, you can infer that the Twenty-first Amendment gave Americans the right to

   (1) drink liquor
   (2) vote for a new President
   (3) pull themselves out of an economic depression
   (4) support Franklin D. Roosevelt's plans

You can look at the earth as divided into three spheres—the atmosphere, the hydrosphere, and the lithosphere. The atmosphere is the air. The atmosphere is made up mostly of gases. About 21% of the atmosphere is oxygen. Another 1% is made up of carbon dioxide and other minor gases, along with water vapor and dust particles. The rest of the atmosphere is made up of nitrogen gas.

Oceans, lakes, rivers, and other bodies of water make up the hydrosphere. The water vapor in the atmosphere is also a part of the hydrosphere.

The lithosphere is the solid part of the earth. The top layer of the earth is the crust. The crust supports all life on earth. It is about 10 to 20 miles deep. Directly beneath the earth's crust is the mantle. Under the mantle is the earth's core, the center of the earth.

7. From the information in the passage, you can infer that most of the earth's atmosphere is made up of

   (1) oxygen
   (2) carbon dioxide
   (3) water vapor and dust particles
   (4) nitrogen

8. The passage implies that the word *hydrosphere* refers to all of the earth's

   (1) gases   (3) oxygen
   (2) water   (4) solids

9. From the information in the passage, you can infer that the earth's surface is part of the earth's

   (1) crust   (3) core
   (2) mantle   (4) atmosphere

Check your answers on page 130.

UNIT REVIEW

In this unit, you've worked on making basic inferences about the details of a passage. Making an inference is a basic thinking and reading skill. When you make an inference, you figure something out. You use the details that are stated in the passage as evidence. You use the evidence to figure out details that aren't stated directly. You've also worked on answering inference questions in this unit. You've worked on strategies to make inference questions easier to answer.

In the next unit, you'll continue to work on building your inference skills. You'll work on making inferences about how details are organized in a passage.

CLOSE-UP ON SCIENCE

In this unit, you read a few science passages. First, you read a passage about nuclear power plants and earthquakes. Then you read a passage about different types of rock. Finally, you read a passage about the three spheres of the earth. All of these passages deal with a branch of science known as **earth science.**

Earth science is the study of the earth. It's also the study of the relationship of the earth to other bodies in space. **Geology** is one branch of earth science. Geology is the study of the earth's structure and history. **Meteorology** is the study of the earth's atmosphere. **Oceanography** is the study of the sea. **Astronomy** is the study of the planets and stars.

Try It: Close-up on Science

The following words are from science passages in this unit. Fill in the blanks in the sentences with the correct words from the list.

atmosphere   hydrosphere   fault   igneous
lithosphere   metamorphic   sedimentary

1. A _____ is a place where parts of the earth come together, like the pieces of a jigsaw puzzle.

2. _____ rock is formed when liquid rock cools and hardens.

3. _____ rock is formed from dirt and sand.

4. _____ rock is rock that has had its chemical makeup or texture changed beneath the earth's surface.

5. The earth's _____ is made up mostly of gases.

6. Oceans, lakes, rivers, and other bodies of water make up the earth's _____ .

7. The _____ is the solid part of the earth.

Check your answers on page 131.

CLOSE-UP ON SOCIAL STUDIES

In this unit, you read a few passages about the past. The passages that you read were about America's **history.** History is a branch of social studies. It is the study of the past.

The history of the United States is short compared with some other countries. But there are important periods of American history. The **Colonial period** covers the years that America was a land of European colonies. The Colonial period covers the years 1500 to 1775. The **Revolutionary period** covers the years of America's war for independence from Great Britain. The Revolutionary War was fought from 1776 to 1783. The period from about 1800 to 1850 is known as the **Age of Expansion.** During those years, the United States grew from a land of 13 Eastern states to a nation that stretched from the Atlantic Ocean to the Pacific. The period from 1860 to 1865 is the **Civil War era.** The years after the Civil War are known as the **Gilded Age.** During the Gilded Age, many of America's big industries were born. The years since 1900 have been marked mostly by wars. **World War I** took place from 1914 to 1918. The 1920s were years of wealth, but they were followed by the **Great Depression** of the 1930s. **World War II** was fought from 1939 to 1945. The years after World War II have been marked by a **"cold" war** (a war of words) with Communist nations, and by wars in Korea (1950 to 1953) and Vietnam (1961 to 1973).

Try It: Close-up on Social Studies

The left-hand column contains words and phrases from the "close-up" and the social studies passages in this unit. Match each word on the left to its meaning on the right.

1. _____ Articles of Confederation

    a.   period of economic problems in the 1930s

2. _____ Civil War

    b.   the first national law of the United States

3. _____ Great Depression

    c.   America's war for independence from Great Britain

4. _____ Louisiana Purchase

    d.   land bought from France in 1803

5. _____ Revolutionary War

    e.   the war between the North and the South

Check your answers on page 132.

CLOSE-UP ON LITERATURE

In this unit, you read some passages of **commentary**. Commentary is writing *about* literature and the arts. There are different kinds of commentary, and this unit includes several of them. Commentary includes writing about television, film, plays, dance, and music. It also includes writing about painting, sculpture, and photography. Commentary can also be writing about literature, such as poetry, fiction, nonfiction, or drama.

Commentary is written for one of two reasons. Sometimes a piece of commentary may only provide a description of its subject. For example, a book review may describe what a book is about, the number of pages in it, whether there are illustrations, etc. Often, though, a review also gives an opinion. For example, the critic may comment on whether a book is well-written, thorough, and complete. When you read examples of commentary, remember these two basic differences in how commentary is written. If a review contains criticisms, being aware of the writer's point of view helps you to a better understanding of the review.

Try It: Close-up on Literature

The following words are from the passage above. Fill in the blanks in the sentences with the correct words from the list.

review   critic   commentary   literature

1. Poetry and fiction are called _____.

2. A _____ of a play may include an account and criticism of it.

3. Writing about literature and the arts is called _____.

4. _____ is the term for a writer whose reviews contain his opinions.

Check your answers on page 132.

ANSWERS AND EXPLANATIONS

Try It: What Is an Inference?

1. You can infer that new television shows are being described and reviewed here. The passage refers to new show, prime time, a network, and the new season. These are all clues that this passage is about new television shows.

2. You can infer that a new series of plays is being described and reviewed here. The passage refers to acting, actors, actresses, drama, and plays. In addition, the writer makes it clear that he was sitting in an actual theater. These are all clues that this passage is about a new series of plays.

Try It: Using Details to Make Inferences

1. You can infer that "Pacific Gas and Electric" is the name of a power company. The first sentence tells you that Pacific Gas and Electric began building a nuclear power plant. The third sentence says that the company said the plant would allow it to provide cheap power to the area. From these details, you can figure out that Pacific Gas and Electric is a power company.

2. You can infer that the people who were against the nuclear plant were afraid that an earthquake would destroy it. The first paragraph tells you that the plant was located only 2½ miles from a fault. It tells you what a fault is and that earthquakes often occur at faults. From this information, you can infer that the people were afraid that an earthquake would hit the plant.

3. You can infer that the Nuclear Regulatory Commission shut down the Diablo Canyon plant because it was dangerous. The last paragraph tells you that the commission shut down the plant. It shut down the plant because there had been a "serious breakdown" in safety at the plant. This decision came after the power company admitted that some dangerous parts of the plant could not survive an earthquake. From these details, you can infer that the plant was shut down because it was dangerous.

4. You can infer that the South won the first battle of Bull Run. The beginning of the second paragraph gives the details to make this inference. It says that, at first, the South's strong military leadership was able to overcome the North's advantages. It says that the first battle of Bull Run showed that the South had much better military leadership. You can infer that, in the battle, the South beat the North.

5. You can infer that the Civil War ended on April 9, 1865. The passage states that the superior resources of the North led to General Lee's surrender. It gives the date of the surrender. You can infer that this is the date on which the war ended.

6. You can infer that the Civil War began in 1861. You've inferred that the war ended in 1865. The first sentence of the passage tells you that the war lasted for four years. Four years before 1865 was 1861.

7. The author suggests that Wright was producing this collection of sculptures from 1876 to 1885. You can infer this from several details. The letters make it clear that Wright had created the sculptures during the period he had vanished from the public eye. The passage says the years 1876 to 1885 were a total blank.

8. You can infer that Brancusi and Moore were sculptors and that they were master sculptors of the twentieth century. You can infer this because they are called "masters of the future." Also the writer compares Wright's sculptures to Brancusi and Moore's work, so you can infer their work included sculpture.

Try It: Answering Inference Questions

1. (3) The first paragraph says that the dance dramatizes the struggle by blacks to win the rights enjoyed by whites. Therefore, you can infer that the two groups of dancers represent blacks and whites. You can eliminate the other answer choices, as no details about them are given.

2. (4) At the end of the dance, the dancers "mingled together." You can infer that, since the dancers represent blacks and whites, the dance implies that blacks and whites begin to mingle together.

3. (2) At the end of the review, the writer praises the dance as "beautiful, graceful, and powerful." The writer says that the dancers moved boldly or slowly, not that the dance itself was bold or slow. The dance dramatizes the civil rights struggle, but the writer does not say it is too dramatic.

4. (2) You can infer that America was in an economic depression. Look at the details in the second paragraph. The second paragraph tells you that Roosevelt carried out a number of bold steps. Each step was designed to pull America out of economic depression. You can infer from this that America was in an economic depression when Roosevelt became President in 1933.

5. (4) You can infer that Roosevelt's steps were NOT conservative. The first paragraph tells you that Roosevelt had promised to change the conservative policies of Herbert C. Hoover. You can infer from this that Roosevelt's steps were not conservative.

6. (1) You can infer that the Twenty-first Amendment gave Americans the right to drink liquor. Look at the details in the third paragraph. The third paragraph says that the amendment did away with the nation's prohibition law. It says that Americans were able to drink liquor legally for the first time since 1920. You can infer that the amendment gave Americans the right to drink liquor.

7. **(4)** You can infer that most of the earth's atmosphere is made up of nitrogen. The first paragraph tells you about the gases in the atmosphere. It says that 21% of the atmosphere is made up of oxygen, and 1% is made up of carbon dioxide, other gases, water vapor and dust particles. It says that the rest of the atmosphere is made up of nitrogen gas. The other gases only make up a total of 22% of the air. Take 22% away from 100%. (100% of something is the whole thing.) Nitrogen makes up 78% of the atmosphere.

8. **(2)** The passage implies that the word *hydrosphere* refers to all of the earth's water. The second paragraph tells you about the hydrosphere. It says that the hydrosphere is made up of oceans, lakes, rivers, other bodies of water, and water vapor. All the things in the hydrosphere are water. Therefore, you can infer that the word *hydrosphere* refers to all of the earth's water.

9. **(1)** You can infer that the earth's surface is part of the earth's crust. Look at the details of the third paragraph. The paragraph says that the top layer of the earth is the crust. The crust supports all life on earth. From these two details, you can infer that the earth's surface is part of the crust.

Try It: Close-up on Science

1. A **fault** is a place where parts of the earth come together, like the pieces of a jigsaw puzzle. This information is given in the passage on page 119.

2. **Igneous** rock is formed when liquid rock cools and hardens. This information is given in the passage on page 122.

3. **Sedimentary** rock is formed from dirt and sand. This information is given in the passage on page 122.

4. **Metamorphic** rock is rock that has had its chemical makeup or texture changed beneath the earth's surface. This information is given in the passage on page 122.

5. The earth's **atmosphere** is made up mostly of gases. This information is given in the passage on page 124.

6. Oceans, lakes, rivers, and other bodies of water make up the earth's **hydrosphere**. This information is given in the passage on page 125.

7. The **lithosphere** is the solid part of the earth. This information is given in the passage on page 125.

Try It: Close-up on Social Studies

1. __b__ The Articles of Confederation were the first national law of the United States. Information about the Articles of Confederation is given in the passage on page 118.

2. __e__ The Civil War was the war between the North and the South. Information about the Civil War is given in the passage on page 120.

3. __a__ The Great Depression was the period of economic problems in the 1930s. Information about the Great Depression is given in the passage on pages 124 and 127.

4. __d__ The Louisiana Purchase was land bought from France in 1803. Information about the Louisiana Purchase is given in the passage on page 118.

5. __c__ The Revolutionary War was America's war for independence from Great Britain. Information about the Revolutionary War is given in the passage on page 127.

Try It: Close-up on Literature

1. Poetry and fiction are called **literature**.

2. A **review** of a play may include an account and criticism of it.

3. Writing about literature and the arts is called **commentary**.

4. **Critic** is the term for a writer whose reviews contain his opinions.

UNIT 8: USING ORGANIZATION TO MAKE INFERENCES

In the last unit, you worked on making basic inferences. You worked on figuring out details that weren't stated in a passage. In this unit, you'll continue to build your inference skills. In this unit, you'll focus on using the organization of details to make inferences.

LOOKING AT ORGANIZATION

In Unit 5 of this book, you worked on finding details that are stated in a passage. You looked at some basic ways in which details are organized: time order, cause, comparison, and classification. In Unit 5, you worked on using key words to find out the way in which details are organized. A passage often contains key words that show you how details fit together. But some passages don't have any key words that point out the organization. In some passages, the ways in which details fit together are *implied*. They aren't stated directly. For example, look at this passage:

> Last year was a bad one for Continental Lumber, Inc. The company's earnings dropped by 86%. Fewer new homes were being built. The demand for lumber had dropped sharply.
>
> The company realized that demand for lumber would not be great this year, either. It laid off 40% of its workers. The company's president and vice-president took big pay cuts. The company also cut its production of lumber by 25%.

How are the details in this passage organized? There aren't any key words that point out the organization. But you can see how the details fit together if you think about them. The first paragraph starts off with a statement: Last year was a bad one for Continental Lumber, Inc. The rest of the details tell you what happened last year. They tell you *why* last year was a bad one for the company. The second paragraph also starts off with a statement: The company realized that demand for lumber would not be great this year, either. The rest of the details tell you a few things that the company did. It isn't hard to figure out that the company did these things *because* it expected another bad year. The details in this passage are organized to show the causes of things. There aren't any words in the passage that point this out. But you can use logic to figure out the organization of the passage.

Try It: Looking at Organization

Read the following passages, and then answer the questions.

Last year, Martin moved from his hometown of Spinks, Arizona, to New York City. Spinks has a population of about 3,000. There are 6 police officers in the town. Half of the town's roads aren't even paved. There's one place to buy food in Spinks—Elrod's Hot Dog Hut. New York is a city of more than 7 million people. Police officers number in the thousands. You couldn't find an unpaved road anywhere in the city, although it's almost as hard to find a road that doesn't have its share of potholes. You could eat dinner in New York restaurants for years and not eat in the same place twice.

1. The passage gives details about Spinks, Arizona, and New York City. What are the details used for in the passage?

The President was worried. The latest news about the economy was not good. Unemployment was up by another 1 percent over the last month. The Gross National Product was down from last year's figure. The federal budget deficit was going to be a few billion dollars higher than he had hoped for. Food prices were so low that farmers were threatening to go on strike. There was more trouble in the Middle East—the nation faced another huge increase in oil prices. It seemed like a very good time to take a vacation.

2. What do the details about unemployment, the Gross National Product, the federal budget deficit, food prices, and the Middle East have in common?

Check your answers on page 144.

USING LOGIC TO MAKE INFERENCES

Reading tests like the three found on the GED usually contain inference questions. Often, the inference questions ask you to figure out something about how details are organized. For example, look at the next passage and the question that follows it.

Gravity is a force. It is the pull of a smaller object toward a larger one. You throw a ball into the air. The ball will travel upward for a while. But it will soon come back to earth. The force of the earth's gravity is greater than the force that you used to throw the ball.

The amount of gravitational pull that an object can exert depends on its mass, the amount of material it contains. The amount of gravitational pull can be measured through weight. Suppose an object weighs 100 pounds on earth. If you put that object on the moon, it would weigh about 17 pounds.

From the passage, you can infer that the object weighing 100 pounds on earth would only weigh about 17 pounds on the moon because

(1)   the moon does not have any gravitational pull
(2)   the earth's gravitational pull is stronger than the moon's
(3)   the earth is closer to the sun than the moon is

Look at the question stem. What is it asking? It's asking you to infer something about the weight of the object. You can guess that the details that you need to answer this question are in the second paragraph.

Why would the object that weighs 100 pounds on earth only weigh about 17 pounds on the moon? The second paragraph tells you that the amount of gravitational pull can be measured through weight. The object weighs more on earth than on the moon. What does that tell you? It tells you that the earth must have a stronger gravitational pull than the moon. The object on earth has a greater weight than if it were on the moon.

Now, look at the answer choices to the question. Can you infer answer choice 1 from the information that's given? No, you can't. The passage says that the amount of gravitational pull can be measured through weight. On the moon, the object would weigh about 17 pounds. The object has some weight. That means that the moon must have some gravitational pull. You can eliminate answer choice 1. What about answer choice 3? The passage doesn't mention anything about the sun. It doesn't say the earth is closer to the sun. You can eliminate answer choice 3, also. Answer choice 2 is correct.

Logic is reasoning. When you use logic, you look at the details. You add the details up to come up with an inference. Many times, the inferences answer questions about connections between ideas.

Here is another passage. Read it, and then try to answer the question that follows it.

Two years ago, the Gridley Manufacturing Company had its lowest earnings ever. Two years ago, the productivity of Gridley's workers was also at its lowest point ever. It took 4.7 man-hours for the Gridley company to produce one of its table lamps. Melissa Gridley, president of the company, knew something was wrong.

Melissa Gridley fired all of the company's managers. She brought in efficiency experts to run the company. The experts spotted a few basic problems in the way that the company had been run. They acted to correct the problems. Old machines were replaced or repaired. The company adopted policies that made the workers feel wanted and needed. Last month, the Gridley Manufacturing Company recorded its highest sales figures ever. The productivity of its workers also was 40% greater than it had been two years before.

The passage implies that one of the problems that the Gridley company had two years ago was that

(1) workers were paid too much money
(2) the company employed too many workers
(3) workers did not feel wanted or needed

This question asks you to identify a problem that the Gridley company had two years ago. The passage doesn't state what the problems were. But you could use logic to figure out what the problems were.

Look at the second paragraph. The second paragraph says that Melissa Gridley brought in some efficiency experts. The experts found some problems. They acted to correct the problems. The passage then tells you what the experts did. It gives you the solutions to the problems. You could figure out what the problems were by looking at the solutions.

The first solution was that old machines were replaced or repaired. From this, you can infer one of the problems. You can infer that some of the Gridley company's machines were old and needed to be fixed or replaced. The next solution was that the company adopted policies that made the workers feel wanted and needed. From this, you can infer that the workers did *not* feel wanted and needed.

Now, look at the answer choices. Does any choice match the problem that you figured out? Answer choice 3 does. Answer choice 3 is the correct answer.

Try It: Using Logic to Make Inferences

Here are two more passages. Read each passage, and then answer the questions about it.

A 24-ounce bottle of All-Brand ketchup costs 89¢. A 24-ounce bottle of Grandma Smith's ketchup costs $1.09. Both brands of ketchup are made by the Frithum Food Company in Salsa Valley, California. In fact, the Frithum Food Company uses the *exact same* ketchup for both brands. Frithum sells three times as many bottles of Grandma Smith's ketchup as All-Brand ketchup.

Grandma Smith's ketchup is nationally advertised. Last year, Frithum spent more than $1 million on ads for Grandma Smith's ketchup. All-Brand ketchup is not advertised at all. All-Brand is sold in the same number of stores as Grandma Smith's ketchup, but it doesn't sell nearly as well.

Frank Tonno, president of the Frithum Food Company, is pleased with the sales figures of both products. "We use the Grandma Smith label for people who like to buy things that are advertised," Tonno said. "We use All-Brand for people who are looking for a bargain." With the two brands of ketchup, Frithum makes about $42 million a year.

1. The passage implies that Grandma Smith's ketchup sells more than All-Brand ketchup because

   (1) Grandma Smith's ketchup tastes better
   (2) Grandma Smith's ketchup is cheaper
   (3) Grandma Smith's ketchup has a nice label
   (4) Grandma Smith's ketchup is advertised

2. Which of the following statements about the two brands of ketchup can be inferred based on the information in the passage?

   (1) The only difference between a bottle of Grandma Smith's ketchup and a bottle of All-Brand ketchup is in the label and the price.
   (2) More people buy Grandma Smith's ketchup because it is better than All-Brand ketchup.
   (3) Most people who buy All-Brand ketchup buy it because of advertising.
   (4) The Frithum Food Company doesn't understand why one brand of ketchup sells better than the other.

Sound is a form of energy. It travels through the air in waves. The waves are called vibrations.

Suppose you drop a book on a table. When the book hits the table, it creates a force. This force acts on the air around it. It causes the air to vibrate. The vibrations occur in waves. (They are like the waves in a pool of water when you throw a rock into it.) The sound waves travel through the air. They act as a force on your eardrum. Your brain recognizes the force as sound.

A vacuum is an empty space that does not contain any air. Suppose a book was dropped on a table in a vacuum. The book would create a force when it hit the table, but it would not create any sound.

3. The passage implies that sound is created by

   (1) waves
   (2) force
   (3) air
   (4) vibrations

4. From the passage, you can infer that the book would not create a sound in a vacuum because

   (1) force cannot be created in a vacuum
   (2) there is no air to vibrate in the vacuum
   (3) there is no gravity in a vacuum
   (4) energy cannot exist in a vacuum

Check your answers on page 144.

APPLYING IDEAS TO ANSWER QUESTIONS

Most inference questions ask you to make inferences about details that are missing from a passage. But there's another kind of inference question that you should know about. Read the following passage, and then go on to the question that follows it.

Suppose you roll a ball along the floor. The ball will roll for a while, but it will eventually stop. Why does it stop? The answer to this question can be found in the first law of motion. The three laws of motion were developed by Isaac Newton in the 1600's. The first law of motion states that an object will remain at rest or move at a constant speed unless it is acted upon by a force. When you roll an object across a floor, two forces act on it to cause it to stop. The first force is gravity. Gravity is the pull of the earth. The second force is friction. Friction is a force of resistance. The amount of friction that is exerted on the object depends on a number of things. One of the things is the smoothness of the surface on which the object is rolled. The smoother the surface, the less friction exerted.

Two 6-ounce hockey pucks are pushed across two different surfaces. The first puck is pushed across a wool rug. The second puck is pushed across a sheet of ice. The same amount of force is used to push both pucks. Based on the information in the passage, which of the following will probably happen?

(1) The first puck will not move forward.
(2) The second puck will not stop unless it hits another object.
(3) The second puck will travel farther than the first puck.

You probably noticed that this question is a lot longer than most of the questions you've seen so far. This question asks you to take the information in the passage and *apply* it to a problem. The question gives you the problem. You have to use the information in the passage to solve the problem.

Look at the question stem. The stem gives you the problem. Two hockey pucks are pushed across two different surfaces. Both pucks weigh the same. The first puck is pushed across a wool rug. The second one is pushed across a sheet of ice. The same amount of force is used to push both pucks.

What will probably happen? To find the answer, you have to apply the information in the passage to the problem. The passage tells you that two forces act on an object to cause it to stop when it is moving across a surface. The first force is gravity. The second force is friction. The passage explains that the smoothness of the surface affects the force of friction. A smoother surface exerts less friction on the object. You can infer from this that an object will travel farther on a smooth surface. Which is smoother, a wool rug or a sheet of ice? From experience, you know that a sheet of ice is smoother than a wool rug. Therefore, the puck that is pushed on the ice will travel farther than the other puck.

Now, look at the answer choices. Does one of the choices match your answer? Answer choice 3 does. It's the correct answer to the question. Just to make sure that you're right, look at the other two choices. Neither one is supported by the information in the passage.

Questions that ask you to apply the information in a passage to a problem are longer than most reading questions. But they're not very hard to answer. All you have to do is understand what the passage is saying. You take the information that the passage gives you and use it to solve a problem.

Try It: Applying Ideas to Answer Questions

Here is another passage. Read it, and then answer the question about it.

There are many factors that affect the price of a product that you buy. The first factor is the amount of money that it costs to produce the product. This includes the cost of material, labor, and shipping. Another factor is competition. Suppose two different companies produce the exact same kind of product. Company A charges less for its product than Company B does. More people will buy Company A's product. This kind of competition helps to keep prices as low as possible.

Another factor that affects price is called elasticity. Elasticity refers to the effect that the price has on how much of the product consumers buy. A product is elastic if its price has little or no effect on its sale. An example of an elastic product is gasoline. In the early 1970's, the price of gasoline nearly doubled. But the amount of gasoline that consumers bought did not decrease. A product is inelastic if its price has a great effect on its sale.

1. Last year, the price of a new Gonza car was $7,300. Last year, 175,000 Gonzas were sold. This year, the price of a new Gonza was raised to $9,200. This year, only 55,000 Gonzas were sold. Based on the information in the passage, which of the following statements describes the Gonza?

    (1) The price of a Gonza is competitive.
    (2) The Gonza is an elastic product.
    (3) The Gonza is an inelastic product.
    (4) The Gonza is a high-quality car.

Check your answer on page 145.

UNIT REVIEW

In this unit, you've worked on using organization to make inferences about the details in a passage. You've worked on using the ways in which details are put together to make inferences. You've worked on using logic to figure out how details are connected to one another. You've also worked on answering questions that ask you to apply information in a passage to an outside problem.

In the next unit, you'll continue to work on using logic to answer questions. You'll work on making logical conclusions about the information that's given in a passage.

CLOSE-UP ON SCIENCE

In this unit, you read passages about gravity, sound, and friction. All of these passages relate to a branch of science called **physics**.

Physics is a science that is based on logic. A physicist studies how and why things happen. What causes an object to move? What causes an object to stop moving? How much energy is needed to make something move? What is electricity, and how does it work? The answers to these questions all involve the study of physics.

Physics is a branch of science that is related to all the other branches. There's a little bit of biology, chemistry, and earth science in physics. The logic of physics is an important part of all branches of science.

Try It: Close-up on Science

The following words are from science passages in this unit. Fill in the blanks in the sentences with the correct words from the list.

energy
gravity
mass
vacuum
weight

1. _____ is the pull of a smaller object toward a larger one.

2. The _____ of an object is the amount of material that it contains.

3. The amount of gravitational pull that the earth has is measured through _____.

4. Sound is a form of _____.

5. A _____ is an empty space that doesn't contain any air.

Check your answers on page 145.

CLOSE-UP ON SOCIAL STUDIES

In this unit, you read some passages about businesses, the economy, and prices. These passages are a part of the branch of social studies known as **economics**. Economics is the study of how products are made, bought, and sold.

Mathematics plays a big part in economics. Economists study a nation's economy by analyzing statistics. These statistics include such things as unemployment rates, inflation rates, the gross national product, and interest rates. Many of the things that economists study are a big part of everyday life. You hear about them and read about them all the time. You experience them when you go to a supermarket and find that the prices of things have gone up.

There are a lot of different terms that are used in economics. Some of the terms are easy to understand. Some aren't so easy. Reading the business section of a newspaper can help you to get a better understanding of economics. Look for stories that explain basic economic terms and ideas. Use a dictionary or encyclopedia to look up the terms that you don't understand. These types of resources can help you to get a good idea about the basics of economics.

Try It: Close-up on Social Studies

The following words are from social studies passages in this unit. Fill in the blanks in the sentences with the correct words from the list. You may have to look up the meaning of some of the words in a dictionary or encyclopedia.

> competition
> demand
> elasticity
> Gross National Product
> productivity

1. _____ refers to the amount of a product that consumers want to buy.

2. The _____ is the total value of all the products and services that a nation produces in a year.

3. _____ refers to the rate at which workers make products.

4. _____ exists when two or more companies make and sell the same product.

5. _____ refers to the effect that price has on how much of a product consumers buy.

Check your answers on page 145.

ANSWERS AND EXPLANATIONS

Try It: Looking at Organization

1. The details about Spinks, Arizona, and New York City are used to compare the two places. They are used to show you how small Spinks is and how big New York City is.

2. The details about unemployment, the Gross National Product, the federal budget deficit, food prices, and the Middle East are all examples of bad news about the economy. The details are used to support the statement that the latest news about the economy was not good.

Try It: Using Logic to Make Inferences

1. **(4)** The passage implies that Grandma Smith's ketchup sells more than All-Brand ketchup because Grandma Smith's ketchup is advertised. The passage tells you that Grandma Smith's and All-Brand are exactly the same, except for two things: Grandma Smith's costs 20¢ more, and it is nationally advertised. From this, you can infer that Grandma Smith's ketchup sells better because of advertising.

2. **(1)** You can infer that the only difference between a bottle of Grandma Smith's ketchup and a bottle of All-Brand ketchup is in the label and the price. Use the process of elimination to answer this question. The passage tells you that the exact same ketchup is used in both brands. You can eliminate answer choice 2 as the correct answer. The passage also tells you that All-Brand is *not* advertised. Therefore, you can eliminate answer choice 3. From the last paragraph, you can infer that Frithum Foods knows exactly why one brand of ketchup sells better than the other. From this, you can eliminate answer choice 4.

3. **(2)** The passage implies that sound is created by force. This question is a little tougher to answer. But you can use logic to answer it. Look at the second paragraph. It tells you that when the book hits the table, it creates a force. The force acts on the air. The force causes the air to vibrate. The vibrations occur in waves. Without the force, there would be no vibration. There would be no waves. Therefore, you can infer that sound is created by force. Without force, there would be no sound.

4. **(2)** You can infer that the book would not create a sound in the vacuum because there is no air to vibrate in the vacuum. The third paragraph of the passage tells you that a vacuum is an empty space that does not contain any air. It

says that if a book were dropped on a table in a vacuum, the book would still create a force, but it would not create a sound. From this, you can infer that a sound cannot be created unless there is air to vibrate.

Try It: Applying Ideas to Answer Questions

1. (3) From the information in the passage, you can infer that the Gonza is an inelastic product. The passage tells you what an inelastic product is. A product is inelastic if its price has a great effect on its sale. The problem in the question stem tells you that sales of the Gonza dropped a lot after its price had been raised. Therefore, you can infer that the Gonza is an inelastic product.

Try It: Close-up on Science

1. **Gravity** is the pull of a smaller object toward a larger one. This information is given in the passage on page 135.

2. The **mass** of an object is the amount of material that it contains. This information is given in the passage on page 135.

3. The amount of gravitational pull that the earth has is measured through **weight**. This information is given in the passage on page 135.

4. Sound is a form of **energy**. This information is given in the passage on page 138.

5. A **vacuum** is an empty space that doesn't contain any air. This information is given in the passage on page 138.

Try It: Close-up on Social Studies

1. **Demand** refers to the amount of a product that consumers want to buy.

2. The **Gross National Product** is the total value of all the products and services that a nation produces in a year. (The Gross National Product is often referred to as the GNP.)

3. **Productivity** refers to the rate at which workers make a product.

4. **Competition** exists when two or more companies make and sell the same type of product.

5. **Elasticity** refers to the effect that price has on how much of a product consumers buy. This information is given in the passage on page 140.

UNIT 9: DRAWING LOGICAL CONCLUSIONS

In the last few units, you worked on making inferences about the details of a passage. You worked on using the details that are stated in a passage to figure out a detail that is not stated. You worked on using logic to make these inferences.

In this unit, you'll keep on working on making inferences. In this unit, you'll work on drawing logical conclusions about a passage that you read.

WHAT IS A CONCLUSION?

You're walking down the street. It's mid-afternoon. The sky was clear this morning, but now there are big, gray clouds overhead. The clouds are racing across the sun. It was warm this morning, but now it's getting cooler. It's also getting windy. In the distance, you hear thunder.

And you've forgotten your umbrella.

Why is the umbrella important?

You looked around. You looked at the facts:

1. It's getting very cloudy.
2. It's getting cooler.
3. It's getting windy.
4. You hear thunder.

You added up the facts. You came to a conclusion:

5. It's going to rain. And you're going to be needing that umbrella.

To reach a conclusion, you add up details. You look at details. Sometimes, all the information is there. Sometimes, you have to infer details. A conclusion is a logical step. You reach that step by putting details together.

Read this passage. Think about the details. Try to think about a conclusion you can reach:

When 62-year-old Wang was admitted to a Shanghai hospital, he had all the signs of a heart attack. Doctors quickly diagnosed his trouble and tried standard emergency treatment. But the treatment didn't seem to help.

Then they tried an ancient Chinese approach: acupuncture.

Chinese doctors have been using acupuncture on patients undergoing open-heart operations. But they had never used it on a heart attack victim.

Two minutes after the doctors had placed their needles into points in Wang's arms, the pain in his chest eased, and he was able to breathe normally. Fifteen minutes after treatment, the pain was practically gone, and his skin was no longer clammy. There was also a measurable improvement in a reading of Wang's heart activity.

According to this passage, can acupuncture be used to treat a heart attack victim?

This passage gives you information. It tells you about acupuncture. You can infer that acupuncture involves placing needles into points in the body. The passage also gives information about the signs of a heart attack. You can infer that the signs of a heart attack include pain in the chest, abnormal breathing, clammy skin, and unusual heart activity. The passage says that soon after doctors started the acupuncture treatment, the patient's condition improved. You can infer a conclusion: Acupuncture seems to have been used successfully to treat a heart attack victim.

How did you come to this conclusion? You did it in almost the same way you concluded that it was going to rain. You followed these steps:

1. Get the details.
2. Put the details together.
3. Think about the details and what they mean.
4. Decide what the next logical step is.

Try It: What Is a Conclusion?

Read the passage, and answer the question about it.

Many animals, from insects to mammals, signal to each other by giving off chemicals called pheromones. Pheromones influence the behavior of animals of the same species. Pheromones are used for sexual attraction and to signal danger. Some plants produce chemicals called allomones. These chemicals resemble pheromones and attract pollinating insects.

Now scientists have discovered another type of allomone that is used not to attract insects but to repel them. They found this chemical in certain wild potatoes and in aphids. The chemical in aphids is used to signal danger. Aphids normally attack potatoes. But scientists noticed that they did not attack wild potatoes.

Scientists hope to use this chemical to keep aphids from attacking other plants.

1. According to the passage, why don't aphids attack wild potatoes?

Check your answer on page 152.

USING ORGANIZATION TO DRAW A CONCLUSION

You can use the organization of a passage to help you draw a conclusion. A lot of times, the way details are put together will lead you to a conclusion. For example, look at this passage:

According to a study by the National Center for Health Statistics, Americans born last year can expect to live to an average age of 74.5 years. This was up from an average age of 73.8 years two years ago, and it was the highest recorded life expectancy.

The study also estimated the infant mortality rate at 11.2 deaths for each 1,000 live births. This was the lowest annual rate ever in the United States.

The report showed there were 3.7 million births last year, up from 3.6 million the year before and the largest yearly total since 1970.

The agency also reported nearly two million deaths last year, at a rate of 857.6 for every 100,000 Americans. Both figures were down slightly from the previous year.

This passage is about vital statistics. Vital statistics include birth and death rates, along with average life expectancy. The passage tells about vital statistics for last year. Based on the statistics in the passage, what can you conclude?

To answer this, look at how the passage is organized. The details are organized to show a comparison. In each paragraph, the vital statistics for last year are given first. These vital statistics are then compared to previous statistics. Sometimes, the actual previous statistic is given; sometimes, it's only told that there was a change from previous statistics. If you compare the statistics that are given, you can draw this conclusion:

Americans born last year can expect to live longer than those born in any previous year.

Here is another passage. As you read it, think about how the details are organized. See if the organization can help you to draw a conclusion.

At one time or another, nearly everyone experiences difficulty in falling asleep or staying asleep. These two problems are generally known as insomnia. Sometimes, these sleep problems are temporary and seem of no importance. But for some people, insomnia is a critical and long-lasting problem.

In some cases, insomnia may be due to a physical disorder or disease. Worrying over personal problems is often to blame. Too much caffeine, a stimulant found in coffee, tea, and sodas, can be the cause. Some prescription drugs can also interfere with sleep.

What is this passage about?

Based on the information in the passage, which of the following statements about the causes of insomnia can be concluded from the passage?

(1) Insomnia is always caused by a disease.
(2) If a person who has insomnia stops drinking coffee, the insomnia will be cured.
(3) There are a number of different causes of insomnia.

To answer the first question, look at how the passage is organized. The first paragraph gives a definition of insomnia. It says that insomnia is difficulty in falling asleep or in staying asleep. The second paragraph gives some of the causes of insomnia. It is organized to show causes. This passage is about insomnia and its causes.

Now, look at the second question. It asks you to pick the statement that gives a logical conclusion about the passage. The best way to answer a question like this one is to use the process of elimination. You've read the passage, and you know what it's about. Now, read each answer choice to find the one that gives a logical conclusion about the passage.

Look at answer choice 1. Is it a logical conclusion? From the passage, you know that there are a number of different causes of insomnia. Disease is one of the causes, but it isn't the only one. You can eliminate answer choice 1. Now, look at answer choice 2. Is it a logical conclusion? Again, the passage tells you that drinking coffee is just one cause of insomnia. There are others. You can infer that coffee is not the only cause of insomnia. You may have been told before that coffee can keep you from sleeping. You may have seen TV commercials that tell you this. But the conclusion that you make should be based on the information in the passage. And the passage tells you that coffee is only one cause of insomnia. Therefore, you can eliminate answer choice 2.

This leaves answer choice 3. Answer choice 3 says that there are a number of different causes of insomnia. This is a logical conclusion to make based on the information in the passage. The details are organized to show you that there are different causes of insomnia. Answer choice 3 is correct.

A conclusion is a logical step. To reach that logical step, look at the details of a passage. See how they are organized. The organization of a passage can lead to a logical conclusion.

Try It: Using Organization to Draw a Conclusion

Here are two more passages. Read each passage. As you read, look at how the passage's details are organized. See if you can use the organization to draw a conclusion. Then answer the questions that follow each passage.

The cost of running electric appliances in your home varies from one season to another. The average cost for running a refrigerator/freezer in the winter, for example, is about 53 cents a day. During the summer, however, the average cost is 56 cents a day.

A color television set can cost an average 4.8 cents an hour in winter months, while summer months show an average cost of 5.1 cents an hour. Washing machine use ranges from 43.1 cents a load in the winter to 45.5 cents a load in the summer. Even the cost of running that electric clock varies—28.7 cents a month in the winter season to 30.4 cents a month in the summer.

1. According to the passage, how much does it cost to run a color television set in the summer?

2. According to the passage, how much does it cost to run a washing machine in the winter?

3. Which of the following statements about the cost of running appliances can you conclude from the passage?

    (1) Refrigerator/freezers are more expensive to run than any other appliance.
    (2) It costs more to run appliances in the summer than in the winter.
    (3) It costs more to run appliances in the winter than in the summer.

    The number of illegal aliens crossing the U.S.-Mexico border has become a torrent, according to officials of the U.S. Border Patrol.
    So far this year, the number of deportable aliens captured and returned to Mexico is up almost 50 percent from last year. In February alone, 80,310 people were caught and sent back.
    One reason for this surge has been the crisis in the Mexican economy. The peso was devalued. This made American money more valuable in Mexico.
    U.S. government officials see little improvement in the Mexican economy over the next few years.

4. What is the passage about?

5. According to the passage, what was one of the major reasons for the increase in the number of illegal aliens?

6. Based on the information in the passage, you can conclude that the number of illegal aliens from Mexico can be expected to

    (1) decrease over the next few years
    (2) remain high over the next few years
    (3) affect the value of the peso

Check your answers on page 152.

UNIT REVIEW

In this unit, you've worked on **drawing conclusions.** You've seen that a conclusion is a logical step. You reach this logical step by looking at the details. You've seen that understanding the organization of details can help you draw a conclusion.

ANSWERS AND EXPLANATIONS

Try It: What Is a Conclusion?

1. The passage tells about pheromones and allomones. It explains that these are chemicals that are used as signals by insects, animals, and plants. The second paragraph tells about a type of allomone that has been discovered. This chemical appears in aphids and wild potatoes. Aphids use the chemical to warn other aphids about danger. Since aphids don't attack wild potatoes, you can conclude that scientists believe that the wild potato gives off this same allomone. You can conclude that wild potatoes fool aphids with this allomone.

Try It: Using Organization to Draw a Conclusion

1. The passage tells about the difference in costs for running electric appliances. The passage compares the costs for the winter and summer. The second paragraph says that the average cost for running a color television set is 5.1 cents an hour in the summer.

2. The second paragraph says that it costs 43.1 cents a load to run a washing machine in the winter.

3. (2) This passage compares costs of running appliances in the winter and summer. Use the process of elimination to answer this question. Answer choice 1 is not supported by the passage; you are not given enough information in the passage to support this conclusion. Answer choices 2 and 3 ask you to compare costs and draw a conclusion. If you look at the average costs that are given for the different appliances, you see that the costs for the summer are greater than the costs for the winter. Answer choice 2 is correct.

4. The passage tells about the number of illegal aliens entering the U.S. from Mexico. The second paragraph says that the number of aliens is up almost 50 percent from last year. The third paragraph gives one reason for the increase in illegal aliens.

5. The third paragraph says that one reason for the increase is the crisis in the Mexican economy. The crisis was brought about by the devaluation of the peso.

6. **(2)** To answer this question, you must infer that a trend in increasing number of aliens will continue. Use the process of elimination. Answer choice 1 says that the number of aliens will decrease. The passage says that one reason for the increase in aliens is the bad Mexican economy. The last paragraph says that U.S. officials do not expect any improvement in the Mexican economy over the next few years. You can infer that the number of aliens is expected to remain high during this time. Answer choice 1 is incorrect. Answer choice 3 is not supported by the passage. Answer choice 2 is correct.

Analyzing What You Read

In the last two sections, you have worked on finding details that are stated in a passsage and making inferences about details that are not stated. There are other kinds of skills to use when you read. Many of those other skills involve analyzing what you read. When you analyze something, you look at all its parts and how they relate to each other.

Analyzing is a large part of the GED. By learning to analyze passages, you will improve your scores on the GED or on any reading test you take.

UNIT 10: RECOGNIZING FACTS AND OPINIONS

Look at these two statements:

Flash, the latest car from Modern Motors, has power steering and power brakes.

The new Flash from Modern Motors is the most comfortable car you'll ever drive.

Both of the statements are about Flash, a new car. But the statements are different in one important way. The first statement gives you a **fact**. The author could prove that the car has power steering and power brakes. Everyone who examines the car could agree that it has these things. But would everyone agree that the Flash is the most comfortable car ever made? No, they probably wouldn't. The second statement is an **opinion**. The author couldn't prove that it was true.

On the Social Studies and Science Tests of the GED, you may be asked to decide if a statement is a fact or an opinion. You may have to decide if the author is reporting information, or if the author is expressing feelings and thoughts about something. In this unit, you'll work on recognizing statements that are facts and statements that are opinions.

USING CLUES TO RECOGNIZE OPINIONS

Often, the same topic can be presented with either facts or opinions. For example, look at the next two passages. They are both about the same concert. But the ways the passages are done are different.

Last night at the Arena in Bayfield, Wallace Richards closed his cross-country tour. The 40-year-old singer performed for three hours before a crowd of 10,000 fans. He sang many of his old hits and surprised the audience with a new song called "Crosswords." Bayfield was the last stop on a six-month tour that included New York, Chicago, and Denver.

I believe that Wallace Richards gave the performance of his life last night at the Arena in Bayfield. It seems that Richards' cross-country tour has been a good experience for the singer. In my opinion, his old hits sounded better than ever. And I think the singer's latest tune, "Crosswords," will put him on the charts once again.

Which passage contains mostly facts about the concert? Which passage contains mostly opinions about the concert?

It's pretty easy to see that the first passage contains facts. It gives you details about the concert. It answers *who, what, when,* and *where* questions. The writer can prove that these details are true. He can prove that they're facts.

In the second passage, the writer gives you some facts. He tells you who sang, where he sang, and what he sang. But it's pretty easy to see that the second passage contains a lot of opinions. Look at the second passage again. Notice the words that tell you that the writer is stating his feelings about the concert:

I believe that Wallace Richards gave the performance of his life last night at the Arena in Bayfield. **It seems** that Richards' cross-country tour has been a good experience for the singer. **In my opinion**, his old hits sounded better than ever. And **I think** the singer's latest tune, "Crosswords," will put him on the charts once again.

The writer begins the first sentence by saying "I believe." Those words tell you that an opinion is coming up. The writer couldn't prove that Wallace Richards gave the performance of his life. Some people might disagree with him. The statement isn't a fact. It's the writer's own belief or opinion. There are other words in the passage that also clue you that an opinion is being stated. The words *it seems, in my opinion,* and *I think* point to an opinion. They tell you that the author is giving you his feelings about the concert.

When you read, look for words like *I think, I believe, I feel,* and *it seems, it appears, it may be.* These words make it easier to spot opinions.

Try It: Using Clues to Recognize Opinions

Read the next two passages. As you read, underline any words that point to an opinion. Answer the questions that follow the passages.

Passage A

Last night, I ate at the Captain's Deck. I thought that the service was too slow and the dining room was too noisy. It appeared that even the cook was having a bad night. I believe that my meal, the seafood platter, had been sitting on the stove for a week. Dinner for two came to $60.00. I feel that at that price, a customer deserves the best. In my opinion, the Captain's Deck is the worst.

Passage B

A new restaurant called the Captain's Deck opened in town last Monday. Located at 4th and Main, the restaurant is run by Ted Lenox. The menu features seafood, but there are also chicken and meat dishes. The house specialty, a seafood platter, costs $25.00. The restaurant is open from 12–3 and 6–11, Tuesday through Sunday.

1. Which passage contains mostly facts?

2. Which passage contains mostly opinions?

Check your answers on page 163.

UNDERSTANDING PURPOSE

Many times, when a writer gives you his opinion, he wants you to agree with him. He may be trying to persuade you to see things his way. He may be trying to convince you of something. Take another look at this sentence.

The new Flash from Modern Motors is the most comfortable car you'll ever drive.

What is the author's purpose in writing this sentence?

The author's purpose is to persuade you that the Flash is a great car. He's trying to convince you that you'll like this car.

A writer who gives you opinions has a different purpose than a writer who gives you facts. Think about the articles in a newspaper, for example. The purpose of a news story is usually to give you information. News stories usually deal with facts. But the purpose of an editorial is to persuade you about something. Editorials usually deal with opinions.

The following passages are about a law that requires pet owners to muzzle their dogs. As you read each passage, think about the author's purpose. Is the author simply reporting the facts? Or is he giving his opinions? Is he trying to give you straight information? Or is he trying to persuade you to agree with him?

On Thursday night, the Jackson City Council voted down a proposed law that would require pet owners to muzzle their dogs. The law was proposed after five people were bitten by dogs last year. A crowd gathered outside the town hall to learn of the council's decision. Most of the people applauded when the decision was read; however, a few chanted in protest.

On Thursday night, the Jackson City Council refused to pass a law that would require pet owners to muzzle their dogs. In my opinion, this is one of the most foolish decisions the council has ever made. Dogs are wild, savage beasts that must be controlled. I believe that we must put a stop to their atttacks. Until pet owners are forced to muzzle their dogs, it won't be safe to walk the streets of Jackson.

The first writer is simply presenting the facts about the muzzle law. He tells you what it is and why it was proposed. He tells you what the city council decided, and he describes some people's reaction to the vote. The writer doesn't give you his opinion about the law. He just tells you that some people were for it, and others were against it. The writer's purpose in the first passage is to give you information about the proposed law.

In the second passage, however, the writer is not simply reporting on the vote. He's commenting on the city council's decision. He lets you know that he doesn't agree with their vote. In the second passage, the writer's purpose is to persuade you that the muzzle law is necessary. He wants you to share his opinion.

When you're trying to separate fact from opinion, think about the writer's purpose. Is he trying to give you information? Or is he trying to convince you of something? If you can answer these questions, it will be easier to identify facts and opinions.

Try It: Understanding Purpose

Read the following passages and answer the questions that follow them. As you read, try to decide the author's purpose.

The recent assault of a teenage boy, Joe Packer, near Fernwood Park is a matter of public concern. At the time the assault happened, several joggers heard Packer's cries for help. But not one of them stopped to help the boy. Apparently, no one looks out for anybody else anymore. It seems that there isn't an ounce of bravery left in our society. I think that there was more than one criminal at work in Fernwood Park. In my opinion, the people that saw the crime and did nothing are guilty, too.

1. Is the main purpose of this passage to state facts about the crime or to give an opinion about it?

A teenage boy was assaulted when riding his bike near Fernwood Park. The youth, Joe Packer of 110 Fernwood Street, was returning from work when the attack occurred. He was thrown from his bike and was kicked and beaten by a man about 24 years old. The attacker fled the scene with Packer's bicycle. Packer reported that several joggers passed by while the attack was in progress. None of the joggers responded to the youth's cries for help.

2. Is the main purpose of this passage to state facts about the crime or to give an opinion about it?

Check your answers on page 164.

ANSWERING QUESTIONS ABOUT FACTS AND OPINIONS

So far in this unit, you've looked at facts and opinions. You've seen that when a writer gives you a fact, he usually wants to convey information about something. You've seen that when a writer gives you his opinion, he often wants to persuade you to agree with him.

On reading tests, you may be asked questions about the author's purpose and opinions. Read the following passage about a sanitation strike. The questions that come after the passage will help you practice answering questions about purpose and opinions. As you read, think about these things. Is the author reporting facts about the strike, or is he commenting on it? Does he have an opinion about the strike? If he does, what is it?

For the last three weeks, garbage has been piling up on the streets of Rockford. Everyone has been blaming the sanitation workers for this condition. But is it really their fault? I don't think so. In my opinion, the mayor is responsible for the sanitation strike. The workers only want the money and benefits that they deserve. Collecting garbage is a hard, sometimes dangerous job. The last few weeks have shown us how important the sanitation workers are. The mayor should give in to the workers' demands and put an end to this strike.

The main purpose of the passage is to

(1) explain why the mayor doesn't want to give in to the workers' demands
(2) persuade readers to collect their own garbage
(3) convince readers that the sanitation workers deserve better pay and benefits
(4) report on the Rockford sanitation workers' strike

This question asks about the author's main purpose. You can use the process of elimination to answer this question. Before you even look at the choices, you know that the author's main purpose is *not* simply to report the facts. The author gives his opinion throughout the passage. As you look at the choices, you can see right away that answer choices 1 and 4 are wrong. Answer choice 1 and 4 say that the author's main purpose is to explain or report facts. Now, look at answer choices 2 and 3. They say that the author's main purpose is to convince or persuade the reader to agree with his opinion. Only one of the choices is the right answer. Does the author think that people should collect their own garbage (choice 2)? No, he never makes that suggestion. But does the author think that sanitation workers deserve better pay and benefits (choice 3)? Yes, he does. In sentence 6, the author says that the workers deserve better pay and benefits. In the next sentences, he tells why he thinks they deserve these things. Answer choice 3 is the best answer to the question.

When you're given a question about the author's purpose, think about the whole passage. Was the author giving you mostly facts or mostly opinions? If he was giving you mostly facts, look for choices that say the author was *reporting, stating,* or *explaining* certain facts. If he was giving you mostly opinions, look for statements that say that the author was trying to *persuade* or *convince* readers about certain opinions.

Now, answer this question about the passage.

Which of the following best states the author's opinion about the strike?

(1) The sanitation workers are wrong to be on strike.
(2) The mayor is wrong not to end the strike by giving the workers what they want.
(3) The mayor should fire all of the strikers.
(4) The strikers should vote against the mayor in the next election.

The question asks for the author's opinion about the strike. Think for a moment about the subject. Does the author support the workers or the mayor? The author supports the workers. In sentences 6, 7, and 8, the author praises the workers. In sentences 5 and 9, the author speaks against the mayor. Now, look at the choices. Answer choices 1 and 3 are statements that do *not* support the workers. Therefore, they do not state the author's opinion about the strike. Answer choice 4 may support the workers, but it's never suggested in the passage. Answer choice 2, however, *does* state the author's opinion. The author says that the strike is the mayor's fault (sentence 5). He says that the workers deserve to get what they want (sentence 6). He also says that the mayor should end the strike (sentence 9).

When you're given a question about the author's opinion, think about the author's topic. Are there different sides to this topic? Which side does the author take? Answering these questions will make it easier to spot the correct choice.

Try It: Answering Questions About Facts and Opinions

Read the passages on the next page. Then answer the questions that follow each passage.

In the next few days, the state senate will have an important decision to make. Should the driving age be raised from 16 to 18? When I was a young boy living in the country, we didn't worry about things like driving ages. At age 13, I was behind the wheel helping out my father. Nobody ever thought twice about my age. It's true that driving is a big responsibility. But people have to be taught to handle responsibility. It doesn't just happen when they turn 18. I say, let the 16 year olds drive. Let them start to help out their parents. Let them begin to take care of themselves.

1. The main purpose of the passage is to

   (1) report on the proposed change in the driving age
   (2) describe the author's childhood
   (3) explain why the government wants to raise the driving age
   (4) persuade readers that the driving age shouldn't be raised

2. Which of the following best states the author's opinion about the driving age?

   (1) 16 year olds are not mature enough to drive.
   (2) 16 year olds should be allowed to drive.
   (3) 16 year olds should have their own cars.
   (4) 18 year olds make fewer mistakes than 16 year olds.

There's been a lot of talk lately about building a new stadium in Willow Grove. It seems that the Willow Grove football team doesn't want to play in an old stadium anymore. They say that they'll move away if we don't build them a new one. In my opinion, the team is being mighty selfish. There are poor people, school children, and senior citizens who really need our tax dollars. Why should we throw good money away on a stadium? Week after week, the fans faithfully turn out to watch the team lose. Is this the way the fans' loyalty is rewarded? I say to the team: Go ahead and go. We can find another team that doesn't need to be pampered.

3. The main purpose of the passage is to

   (1) urge readers to support the construction of a new stadium
   (2) report on plans to build a new stadium
   (3) convince readers that Willow Grove doesn't need a new stadium
   (4) explain why the team wants to leave Willow Grove

4. Which of the following best states the author's opinion about building a new stadium?

    (1) A new stadium would be good for the economy of Willow Grove.
    (2) Building a new stadium is a waste of money.
    (3) The team would win more games in a new stadium.
    (4) There is nowhere to put a new stadium in Willow Grove.

Check your answers on page 164.

UNIT REVIEW

In this unit, you've worked on separating **facts** from **opinions.** Facts are statements that the author could prove are true. Facts can answer *who, what, where, when, why,* and *how* questions. When the author's purpose is to report on something, he usually presents the facts.

Opinions, however, are statements that can't be proven. Opinions give you the author's beliefs or feelings about something. When the author's purpose is to comment on something, he usually deals in opinions. Often, he tries to persuade you to agree with his opinions.

There are some words that you can look out for when you're separating facts from opinions. Words like *I think, I feel,* and *it seems,* for example, tell you that an opinion is coming up.

In the next unit, you'll take a closer look at how authors use words to persuade you to think a certain way.

ANSWERS AND EXPLANATIONS

Try It: Using Clues to Recognize Opinions

1. The second passage contains mostly facts. The author describes the restaurant, but he doesn't say if he likes it or not. The name of the restaurant and its owner, the day that it opened, its location and hours, its menu, and the price of the seafood platter are all facts from the passage.

2. The first passage contains mostly opinions. The author describes his feelings about the atmosphere, service, food, and price. Other people might disagree with his description of the restaurant. The writer uses the words *I thought, it appeared, I believe, I feel,* and *in my opinion.* These words point to opinions.

Try It: Understanding Purpose

1. The main purpose of the passage is to give an opinion about the crime. The author does not simply report what happened to Joe Packer. He lets you know that he thinks the crime is an example of cowardice in the community. He uses the crime to discuss what he sees as a problem in society.

2. The main purpose of the passage is to state facts about the crime. The author does not comment on the crime. He simply reports the who, what, where, and when of the crime.

Try It: Answering Questions About Facts and Opinions

1. **(4)** The main purpose of the passage is to persuade readers that the driving age shouldn't be raised. The author deals mostly with opinions, not facts. Therefore, answer choices 1 and 3 are incorrect. The author does describe his childhood (answer choice 2), but only to point out that young people are capable of driving. He spends most of the passage arguing against raising the driving age.

2. **(2)** The author believes that 16 year olds should be allowed to drive. In the third sentence, the author says that he drove when he was 13. He says that he helped his father out by driving. In the following sentences, the author says that 16 year olds should be given the responsibility of driving. He implies that the responsibility will be good for them.

3. **(3)** The main purpose of the passage is to convince readers that Willow Grove doesn't need a new stadium. The author deals mostly with opinions, not facts. Therefore, answer choices 2 and 4 are incorrect. The author doesn't think a new stadium should be built (answer choice 1). He thinks a new stadium would be a waste of money (sentence 6).

4. **(2)** The author's opinion is that building a new stadium is a waste of money. He states this opinion in the sixth sentence of the passage.

UNIT 11: IDENTIFYING BIAS AND TONE

In the last unit, you worked on separating facts from opinions. You looked at passages in which the writer stated his opinions directly. Sometimes, though, the writer doesn't come right out and give you his opinions. For example, look at this sentence:

> In the last inning, clumsy Ted Beech let a ball slip right through his hands.

At first it may seem as if the author is simply presenting the facts. The author doesn't state his opinion directly. But the author calls Beech "clumsy." And he doesn't just say that Beech dropped a ball, he says that he "let it slip right through his hands." You can infer that the author doesn't think much of Beech. The author's choice of words shows that he doesn't believe that Beech is a capable ball player.

In this unit, you'll look at opinions that aren't stated directly. You'll work on identifying the author's attitude about his subject. You'll see how the author's choice of words reflects his opinions and attitude.

IDENTIFYING UNSTATED OPINIONS

Suppose that you want to buy a car. You see this sentence in a consumer report:

> The Warbler gets an estimated 20 miles per gallon in highway driving.

Now suppose that you read a brochure from a car maker. This sentence appears in the brochure:

> The money-saving Warbler gets great gas mileage.

Which sentence gives you more unbiased information about the car?

It's pretty easy to see that the first writer gives you unbiased information about the car. The writer gives you straight facts. He doesn't let his opinion enter into his description of the car. He lets the reader decide whether or not 20 miles per gallon is good gas mileage. The second reader, however, gives a biased view of the car's gas mileage. The writer wants you to like the car. He says that its gas mileage is "great," and he calls the car "money-saving." His opinion of the car shows in the words that he uses to describe it. He tries to draw the reader into sharing his opinion of the car.

The next two passages have the same topic—television. But the writers have very different opinions about television. As you read the passage, pay close attention to the words that each author uses to describe television. Try to decide what opinion of television the words reflect.

> In the 1940's, people began to bring a dangerous machine into their homes. This machine was called a TV set. Ever since then, people have been wasting valuable hours staring at the boob tube. They stare at silly sitcoms; they stare at stupid dramas. And as they stare, their eyesight is ruined and their minds are destroyed.

How does the author of this passage feel about television?

Right from the start, it's clear that the author hates television. He calls it a "dangerous machine" and a "boob tube." He describes TV shows as "silly" and "stupid." He says that people "waste valuable hours" when they "stare" at the TV set. The writer accuses TV of "ruining" eyes and "destroying" minds. All of these describing words suggest that TV is bad. They convey the author's negative feelings about his subject. They reveal the author's opinion that TV is harmful.

Now read another author's view of TV and answer the question that follows.

> With a touch of a button, television brings the world into the home of modern man. Through the miracle of television, man can be informed about events in far-off countries. He can be entertained by humorous comedies, or he can be moved by stirring dramas. Television broadens the mind and enriches the lives of people everywhere.

What is this writer's opinion of television?

The author of this passage is clearly in favor of television. He uses words that make television sound like a very good thing. The author calls television a "miracle." He describes TV shows as "humorous" and "stirring." He tells you that people are "informed," "entertained," and "moved" by TV. The writer praises TV for "broadening" the mind and "enriching" life. All of these describing words suggest that TV is a wonderful thing. They convey the author's positive feelings about the subject. They reveal the author's opinion that TV is a great invention.

When you read, notice the words that the author uses to describe his subject. Oftentimes, the author's attitude towards his subject will be revealed by these describing words.

Try It: Identifying Unstated Opinions

Read each passage. Answer the question that follows each passage.

Within the next year, the beauty of Rockgreen Park will be destroyed by the construction of the Rockgreen Mall. After a long battle with land baron Skip Beret, the Rockgreen community lost its cherished park. Beret plans to deposit a 50-store shopping mall on the site. The monstrous structure is certain to bring swarms of shoppers into the once-peaceful area.

1. What is the author's opinion of the shopping mall?

The rebirth of the Rockgreen area will begin with the construction of a new business center, the Rockgreen Mall. Genius land developer Skip Beret plans to create a 50-store shopping wonderland on the abandoned park in the center of town. Local residents are very excited about the mall. Many look to the mall to strengthen the economy of the area.

2. What is this author's opinion of the shopping mall?

Check your answers on page 173.

IDENTIFYING TONE

An author may state his opinions about a subject in a very cool, calm way. Think, for example, about two candidates in a debate. Suppose they are discussing their positions on tax increases. Each one has different opinions, but each presents his opinions with little emotion. Then suppose that the subject turns to nuclear power. Nuclear power is a big issue in the community. The tone of the candidates' debate changes. It becomes emotional. The candidates shout angrily at each other. The tone of the debate reflects the strong feelings that the candidates seem to have about the issue.

Like the tone of a debate, the tone of a passage reflects the author's feelings about his subject. The tone can be angry, humorous, or sad. It can be sympathetic or mocking. There are many different kinds of tones.

The passages that follow are about riding the bus. Each passage is written with a different tone. As you read, think about the author's attitude towards his subject. How does he describe his subject? What feelings do these descriptions suggest?

From my spot in the back of the bus, I could watch the herd of people as they entered the cattle car. Keep on pushing folks, I thought, make sure not to look out for anybody else. By all means, sir, I silently said to the man next to me, don't take that stupid look off your face. In the front of the bus, two old hens began to claw at each other over a seat. A few vultures hovered nearby them, ready for some excitement.

What is the tone of this passage? What is the author's attitude toward his subject?

The author's attitude toward his subject is mocking. He describes the people on the bus as animals by calling them a "herd" and by speaking of a "cattle car." He refers to some of the people as "old hens" and "vultures." He puts himself at a distance from his subject and mocks the way that the people act. He accuses the people on the bus of only caring about themselves. He says that the man next to him has a "stupid" look on his face. All of these descriptions combine to give the passage a mocking tone.

Now, read another passage about a bus.

The group of weary commuters silently boarded the crowded bus. I took a seat next to a middle-aged gentleman whose face told of years of hard work and worries. He had only enough energy left to gaze out the window at the long row of office buildings. In front of

the bus, two women reacted to the day's tension by
quarreling about a seat.

Is the tone of this passage mocking? What is the author's attitude toward his subject?

The tone of this passage is very different from the passage before
it. The author is sympathetic toward the people on the bus. This
author refers to his subject with terms of respect. He calls them
"weary commuters" and speaks of a "gentleman" and "two women."
He says nothing about people pushing each other, and he looks for
reasons why the man stares out the window and the women fight. He
seems to be aware of their troubles and doesn't judge them harshly.
The tone of this passage can best be described as sympathetic.

Here is another passage about riding a bus:

I hopped on the bus with my fellow workers. It was
the weekend! People chatted to each other about the day's
events and grinningly reported their plans for the
holiday. I settled into my seat and dreamed about
swimming in the cool lake and lounging on the beach.

What is the tone of this passage?

The tone of this passage is cheerful. The author speaks affection-
ately about the other riders. He calls them his "fellow workers" and
says that they "chatted" and "grinned." He doesn't describe any un-
pleasant events or unhappy people. The author's attitude toward the
bus ride is cheerful.

The tone of a passage expresses the author's attitude toward his
subject. When you think about tone, consider the passage as a whole.
What kind of feeling does the passage convey? What kinds of describing words does the author use? What kinds of incidents does he relate? Answering these questions will help you identify the tone.

Try It: Identifying Tone

Read each passage. Answer the question that follows each passage.

The sun blazed brightly over the green world. The
boy chewed contentedly at the blade of grass in his
mouth. He lazily swatted a fly that had landed on his
sleeve. He heard the playful sounds of the other boys. He

waited for the batter to arc a ball toward him. He wanted to reach out and grab the ball. He wanted to reach out and grab the sun. Summer was here, and all was good.

1. Is the tone of this passage joyful or depressing?

The book said that you should talk to your plants. In an effort to coax some life from my dry, faded stalks, I decided to try it. Day after day, I found myself whispering to a windowsill of deaf begonias. It didn't seem to work.

Finally, one day I shouted: "That does it. Here I am, watering, pruning and fertilizing a houseful of plants, and what do I get? Not even a green shoot. What do you want from me?"

The begonias rustled: "You could at least maintain proper lighting, adjust the indoor temperature, and use decorative clay pots."

I argued: "I never promised you a rose garden."

One begonia muttered: "Right now, I'd settle for a rock garden."

From now on, I've decided to talk to plastic daisies; at least they don't argue.

2. Is the tone of this passage humorous or serious?

The old man got up at seven. He always got up at seven. That was the time he used to get up for work. There was no reason for him to get up at seven now, but it was a habit.

The old man got dressed. He put on a pair of gray pants and a white shirt. They used to be his work clothes. Now they were just clothes.

The old man went down to the kitchen. He made a cup of instant coffee. He buttered a slice of toast. He sat down at the kitchen table, and waited for the day to go by.

3. Is the author of this passage sympathetic or unsympathetic toward his subject?

Check your answers on page 174.

ANSWERING QUESTIONS ABOUT BIAS AND TONE

Reading tests like the GED Interpreting Literature and the Arts Test often ask questions about bias and tone. One type of bias question often appears. Read the next passage, and then look at the question.

Each year, thousands and thousands of people are run down and murdered by drunk drivers. With every passing year, the statistics on deaths due to drunk driving get more and more grim. And statistics don't even tell part of the story. You can't use statistics to show the grief of a mother whose child has been needlessly run down by a drunk who got behind the wheel. You can't use statistics to show the pain of a young woman who must go through life crippled because of a drunk driver.

With which of the following statements about drunk drivers would the author of the passage most likely agree?

(1) Drunk drivers need understanding.
(2) Drunk drivers can't be blamed for accidents.
(3) Drunk drivers should be severely punished.

What is the question asking? It's asking you to pick a statement that the author of the passage would agree with. To answer this question, you have to identify the author's point of view on the subject of drunk drivers.

What is the author's point of view? From the passage, you can tell that the author is not sympathetic toward drunk drivers. The author says that drunk drivers murder people. Examples are used to show the pain and suffering that drunk drivers cause.

To answer the question, read each answer choice. Which answer choice matches up with the author's point of view and bias? Answer choice 1 doesn't. It says that drunk drivers need understanding. There's nothing in the passage that would lead you to believe that the author agrees with this. Now, look at answer choice 2. From the author's tone, you know for sure that he would not agree with this answer choice. But he would agree with answer choice 3. He would agree that drunk drivers should be severely punished.

Questions about tone are also usually pretty easy to answer. To answer a tone question, the best thing to do is to use the process of elimination. For example, look at this question about the passage that you just read:

The tone of this passage can best be described as

(1) humorous
(2) sympathetic
(3) serious
(4) sarcastic

Look at answer choice 1. Is the tone of the passage humorous? It certainly isn't. Is it sympathetic (answer choice 2)? The author does show sympathy for the victims of drunk drivers. But he isn't sympathetic toward drunk drivers. So you can't say that the tone of the entire passage is sympathetic. However, you could say that it is serious. The author is very serious about his treatment of drunk drivers. Answer choice 3 is correct. To make sure, look at answer choice 4. There's nothing in the passage to suggest that the author is making fun of his topic. The tone of the passage is not sarcastic.

When you answer questions about bias and tone, use the process of elimination. First, read the passage to get an idea of what the author's point of view is. See if the author's choice of words or topic gives you any clue to the tone of the passage. When you answer the question, look at each answer choice carefully. Pick the one that most closely matches your judgment about the bias or tone.

Try It: Answering Questions About Bias and Tone

Here is another passage. Read it, and then answer the questions about it.

Last month, the local town council passed a new law. The law says that if I don't clean up after my dog, I could get a $50 fine. With all the crime and murder going on in town, you'd think that our leaders would have better things to do than this. Obviously, they don't.

At first, I was steamed about the law. But then, a thought came to me. This new law could be the biggest money-maker in a long time! Not for the town, but for me! Since last month, I've been busy working on two new schemes. Both of them are aimed to get money out of people like me—people who don't want to go around picking up their dog's droppings.

Today is the climax of one month's worth of hard work. Today is the day that I open the K-9 Dog Training Institute. The purpose of the institute is to teach dogs to clean up after themselves. For a mere $150, anyone can send his or her dog to me. In three short weeks, I promise that the pooch will be able to clean up after himself. (I'll even issue diplomas—made up of newspapers, of course.)

Today is also the day that I send a letter to the U.S. Patent Office. The patent is for the doggie diapers that I've invented. I expect that, once I get my patent, I'll be able to clean up in the dog dropping market.

Does all this sound a little strange to you? It should. But which is stranger, my ideas or the ideas of our wonderful town council?

1. With which of the following statements about the new law would the author most likely agree?

(1) The new law will help make streets cleaner.
(2) The new law is stupid.
(3) The new law will save people a lot of money.
(4) The new law should have been passed a long time ago.

2. The tone of this passage can best be described as

(1) serious
(2) sympathetic
(3) sarcastic
(4) tense

Check your answers on page 174.

ANSWERS AND EXPLANATIONS

Try It: Identifying Unstated Opinions

1. The author of this passage disapproves of the construction of the shopping mall. He thinks that it is bad for the community. The author calls the mall a "monstrous structure." He says that the developer of the mall is a "land baron." The author talks about how the mall will "destroy" the "beauty" of the "cherished" park and ruin the peace of the community. All of these words suggest that the author is against building a mall on the park.

2. The author of this passage approves of the construction of the shopping mall. He thinks that it is good for the community. The author calls the mall a "business center" and a "wonderland." He says that the developer of the mall is a "genius." The author only briefly mentions that the mall will take the place of a park, and he says that the park is "abandoned." The author says that the mall will start the "rebirth" of the area. He claims that people are "excited" about it. All of these words suggest that the author is for building a mall in Rockgreen.

Try It: Identifying Tone

1. The tone of the passage is joyful. The author describes the beauty of the day and the happiness of the boy. When he says that the boy "wanted to reach out and grab the sun," he dramatizes a feeling of joy.

2. The tone of this passage is humorous. The author jokes about talking to plants.

3. The author of this passage is sympathetic toward his subject. He never criticizes or makes fun of the old man. He describes the reasons for the man's routine. He tries to show you that the man is lonely and bored.

Try It: Answering Questions About Bias and Tone

1. (2) The author would most likely agree with the statement that the new law is stupid. In the first two paragraphs, the author lets you know that he doesn't like the new law. He says that he was "steamed" about it. The author then relates how he will make money from the new law. He makes fun of the law with his two "schemes."

2. (3) The tone of the passage can best be described as sarcastic. The author makes fun of the law by coming up with two silly "schemes." In the last paragraph, he implies that the law is just as silly as his schemes.

Understanding Illustrations

So far in this book, you've learned and practiced skills by reading passages. There are times, though, when ideas are not explained in words. The ideas may be made up of many small details, or the connections between ideas may be very complicated. At such times, writers often use illustrations: tables, graphs, diagrams, and maps.

Understanding illustrations is as important as understanding the passages you read. Illustrations often sum up long stretches of prose. Sometimes illustrations contain facts that are not even in a passage but are necessary if you want to understand what you're reading. If you skip over an illustration, you may miss some important ideas, or may ignore an easy and convenient summary of the materials you are trying to understand.

Before you can use illustrations, you have to know what they are and how they do what they do. In this unit you will look at several kinds of illustrations in detail. You will learn about their different parts, how they hold information, and how you can get information from them. There really *are* times when a picture is worth a thousand words.

UNIT 12: READING TABLES, GRAPHS, DIAGRAMS, AND MAPS

READING TABLES

Writers sometimes use tables to get across ideas that are hard to put into words. Here is an example. Read the passage below.

The history of the Earth is divided into three eras, or periods of time. The era called the Mesozoic (mess oh ZOE ik) came before the era we are now in. It lasted from about 225 million BC (before Christ) to 65 million BC. The Mesozoic is sometimes called "The Age of Reptiles." The era was made up of three periods. During each period certain kinds of animals dominated the Earth. The earliest period was the Triassic (try ASS ik). It lasted from 225 million BC to 195 million BC. The main animals of the time were reptiles such as lizards, frogs, and turtles. The next period, the Jurassic (joo RASS ik), lasted from about 195 million BC to 135 million BC. The first dinosaurs appeared, and the first birds as well. The third period, the Cretaceous (kri TAY shus), lasted from 135 million BC to 65 million BC. Dinosaurs were dominant, but there were also many kinds of birds, and the first true mammals appeared. At the end of the Cretaceous Period, dinosaurs disappeared. The Earth was left to the mammals, which changed slowly over time to the higher forms of life on Earth today.

It is very hard to absorb all the ideas in this passage. They are complicated, and there are too many of them.

Now look at the table below. It has the same information as the passage, but it is arranged in logical order, and all extra words have been left out.

Animals of the Mesozoic Era
The Age of Reptiles
(225 million BC–65 million BC)

Period	Time	Major Animal Life Forms
Triassic	225 million BC to 195 million BC	reptiles: turtles, frogs, lizards
Jurassic	195 million BC to 135 million BC	early dinosaurs, first birds
Cretaceous	135 million BC to 65 million BC	dinosaurs, birds, true mammals

A table is a way of showing facts. The facts are arranged in a way that makes them easy to find.

A table has three parts. The **title** tells what the table is about. The title of the table tells you that it is about Animals of the Mesozoic Era. The **rows** are lines that go across. Each row gives facts about one thing. The top row has labels that describe the information in the columns underneath them. In this table, the labels are Period, Time, and Major Animal Life Forms. The **columns** are lines that run up and down. Each column lists facts. In the example, the columns give details about the period, time, and animal forms.

You find facts in a table by moving *down* a column and *across* a row. A particular fact is located where the line down and line across meet. Use the table to answer the question "What were the major animals on the Earth during the Jurassic period?"

Find the label "Period" at the left of the top row. Now look down the column under the label "Period." Find "Jurassic" in that column. Now look up to the top row again and find the label "Major Animal Life Forms." Draw an imaginary line across from "Jurassic" and another one down from "Major Animal Life Forms." The answer to the question is in the space where the imaginary lines cross. The answer is that the major life forms of the Jurassic were early dinosaurs and the first birds.

You can also move from the information in the table to the top row or to the left column. Use the table to answer the question "Which period ended in 65 million BC?" Find the label "Time" in the top row. Look down that column and find 65 million BC. Now move left to read the period. The answer is that the Cretaceous period ended in 65 million BC.

You can use the table also to find answers to harder questions. Which period lasted the longest? Subtract the two figures in each entry in the Time column. You will find that the Cretaceous lasted longest; it lasted 70 million years. Tables also make it easy to compare information. For example, in this table, you can easily compare the different kinds of animals living in each period.

Try It: Reading Tables

Look at the tables that follow. Then answer the questions about them.

Number of Representatives in Congress

State	Senators	Members of the House	Population (1980 census)
California	2	45	23,668,562
Idaho	2	2	943,935
Kentucky	2	7	3,661,433
New York	2	34	17,557,288
Texas	2	27	14,228,383

Note: Congress is made up of the Senate and the House of Representatives.

1. How many members of the House does Kentucky have?

   (1) 2
   (2) 7
   (3) 34

2. What is the population of New York?

   (1) 17,557,288
   (2) 3,661,433
   (3) 34

3. Which state has a population under 1 million?

   (1) California
   (2) Idaho
   (3) Kentucky

4. The number of senators from any state is

   (1) always 2
   (2) based on the population
   (3) based on the number of members in the House

5. States with large populations have

   (1) more senators than other states
   (2) fewer members of the House than other states
   (3) more members of the House than other states

Recommended Daily Dietary Allowances of 6 Vitamins and Minerals

(amounts in milligrams)

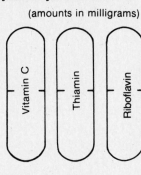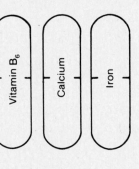

	Vitamin C	Thiamin	Riboflavin	Vitamin B$_6$	Calcium	Iron
Children 7-10 years	45	1.2	1.4	1.6	800	10
Boys 11-14 years	50	1.4	1.6	1.8	1200	18
Girls 11-14 years	50	1.1	1.3	1.8	1200	18
Men (adult)	60	1.4	1.6	2.2	800	10
Women (adult)	60	1.0	1.2	2.0	800	18

6. How many milligrams of Vitamin C does an adult man need daily?

   (1) 45
   (2) 50
   (3) 60

7. According to the table, how many milligrams of iron does a 12-year-old girl need daily?

   (1) 18
   (2) 1.8
   (3) 10

8. Which of the following age groups needs as much calcium daily as girls 11 to 14 years old?

   (1) children 7–10 years old
   (2) boys 11–14 years old
   (3) adult women

9. According to the table, which group needs the most Vitamin B$_6$ daily?

   (1) girls 11–14 years old
   (2) boys 11–14 years old
   (3) adult men

Population, U.S. Cities

	1970	1980
Boston	641,071	562,118
Chicago	3,369,357	3,049,479
Detroit	1,514,063	1,257,879
Houston	1,233,535	1,572,981
Miami	334,859	347,862
New York	7,895,563	7,134,542
Philadelphia	1,949,996	1,680,235
Phoenix	582,500	681,355
St. Louis	622,236	508,496

Note: Figures are based on U.S. census.

10. What was the population of Houston in 1970?

   (1) 1,572,981
   (2) 1,233,535
   (3) 1,514,063

11. Which city had the lowest population in 1980?

   (1) Boston
   (2) St. Louis
   (3) Miami

12. What was the population of Chicago in 1980?

   (1) 3,049,479
   (2) 3,369,357
   (3) 1,257,879

13. Which of the following statements about the populations of U.S. cities can you infer based on the information in the table?

   (1) The populations of U.S. cities decreased from 1970 to 1980.
   (2) The populations of cities in the northern part of the U.S. increased from 1970 to 1980.
   (3) The populations of cities in the Sunbelt (the West and South) increased from 1970 to 1980.

Check your answers on page 199.

READING GRAPHS

Graphs are pictures of facts. They help you compare facts. Some let you see changes over time.

Picture Graphs

There are many different kinds of graphs. Some graphs use pictures to represent things.

Women at Work, 1920–1980

Note: Each symbol represents one million women at work.

Picture graphs have four parts. The **title** tells you the topic of the graph. This graph is about "Women at Work." The **key** tells you what each picture represents. In this graph, one symbol represents one million women at work. The **left column** has labels, to give you details about the graph. In this graph, the left column lists years between 1920 and 1980. Next to each label is a row of **symbols** or **pictures.** In this graph, the symbols show the number of women who worked in that year.

You can use the graph to answer questions. How many women were at work in 1930? Find the year 1930 in the left column. Count the number of figures in the row. There are 10½ figures. Since a figure represents one million women, 10½ million women were at work in 1930.

This picture graph also shows trends—long-term patterns—in the number of women at work. Have more women or fewer women gone to work each year since 1920? You do not need to count to answer this question. A glance at the graph shows you that more women have gone to work each year.

Try It: Reading Picture Graphs

Look at the graph and then answer the questions about it.

U.S. Government Debt 1975–1986

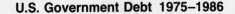

	1 trillion	2 trillion
1975	$ $ $ $ $	
1976	$ $ $ $ $ $	
1977	$ $ $ $ $ $ $	
1978	$ $ $ $ $ $ $ $	
1979	$ $ $ $ $ $ $ $	
1980	$ $ $ $ $ $ $ $ $	
1981	$ $ $ $ $ $ $ $ $ $	
1982	$ $ $ $ $ $ $ $ $ $ $	
1983	$ $ $ $ $ $ $ $ $ $ $ $ $	
1984	$ $ $ $ $ $ $ $ $ $ $ $ $ $	
1985	$ $ $ $ $ $ $ $ $ $ $ $ $ $ $ $	
1986	$ $ $ $ $ $ $ $ $ $ $ $ $ $ $ $ $ $ $	

Note: Each $ = 100 billion dollars of debt.

1. In 1979, the U.S. government debt was

   (1) 800 billion dollars
   (2) 600 billion dollars
   (3) 800 million dollars

2. The debt in 1982 was

   (1) about the same as the 1976 debt
   (2) half as large as the 1976 debt
   (3) almost twice as large as the 1976 debt

3. The trend the chart shows is that government debt has

   (1) increased and then decreased
   (2) not decreased
   (3) decreased and then increased

4. If the trend the chart shows continues, the government debt in 1990 will be

   (1) smaller than in 1986
   (2) the same as in 1986
   (3) larger than in 1986

Check your answers on page 200.

Circle Graphs

A circle graph looks like a circle divided up into pieces. It is also sometimes called a pie chart. The circle represents the whole pie. The lines show the slices that the pie has been cut into. Some pieces may be large, others may be tiny. Altogether, the pieces make up the whole pie. The point of a circle graph is to show what proportion of the whole the different pieces represent and to make it easy to compare them. Put another way, a whole pie must equal 100%, and the percentages that the pieces represent must add up to 100%.

Production of Electricity in the U.S. by Source

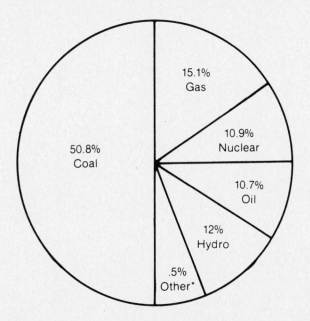

*includes electricity produced from geothermal power, wood, and waste.

A circle graph has five parts. It has a **title**, which tells what the graph is about. It has a **circle**, which represents the whole of something. The circle is cut up into **pieces**; each piece represents part of the whole. Each piece has a **label** that tells what it represents. Sometimes a **footnote** gives further information about a part of the graph.

The graph above shows the different sources of electricity in the United States. Each source is a piece of the circle. The more electricity made by a source, the larger the percentage it contributes and the larger its piece. Altogether, the pieces add up to 100%.

You can use this circle graph to answer questions about sources of electricity. What percent of U.S. electricity is made by nuclear plants? Find the label "Nuclear" in the circle and read the answer: 10.9%.

A circle graph makes it easy to compare quantities. What is the source of most of the electricity in the United States? "Coal" is the largest piece in the circle, so it is the source of the most electricity. What percent of electricity does coal supply? You can tell by looking at the circle. It supplies about half, because its piece is half the circle. You can also read the answer, 50.8%, in the label.

Try It: Reading Circle Graphs

Look at the graph. Then answer the questions.

U.S. Exports, 1980

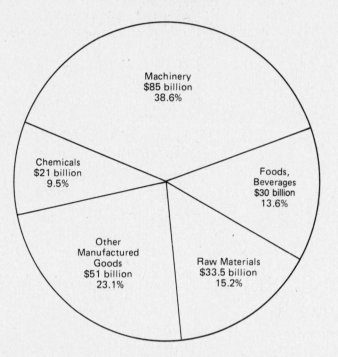

1. U.S. food and beverage exports in 1980 were worth:

   (1) $33.5 billion
   (2) $30 billion
   (3) $13.6 billion

2. Machinery made up what percent of exports in 1980?

   (1) 85%
   (2) 38.6%
   (3) 23.1%

3. Food and beverage exports were worth about the same amount as

   (1) Raw material exports
   (2) Chemical exports
   (3) Machinery exports

4. Based on the graph, you can infer that the United States is mainly

   (1) an agricultural country
   (2) a manufacturing or industrial country
   (3) a mining country

Highest Educational Levels: U.S. Citizens Aged 18–24, 1986

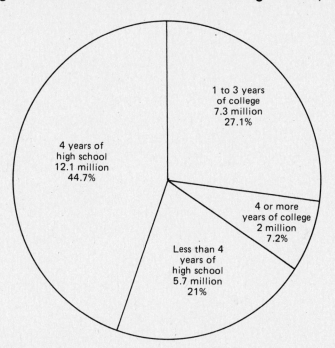

5. What percent of 18–24-year-olds did not get a high school degree?

    (1) 21%
    (2) 5.7%
    (3) 44.7%

6. About how many people end their education after finishing high school?

    (1) about 1 in 5
    (2) about half the people
    (3) about as many as graduate from college

7. Which of these statements is true?

    (1) In 1986 there were more college graduates than high school dropouts.
    (2) Only about a million 18–24-year-olds failed to get a high school degree in 1986.
    (3) The number of high school dropouts was almost 3 times the number of college graduates.

8. If the better jobs go to those with at least a high school education, the graph implies that

    (1) a majority of 18–24-year-olds should get good jobs
    (2) fewer than 1 out of 10 will get good jobs
    (3) a majority of 18–24-year-olds will not get good jobs

Check your answers on page 200.

Bar Graphs

Some graphs use bars to show amounts. They are called bar graphs.

U.S. Casualties in Five Wars

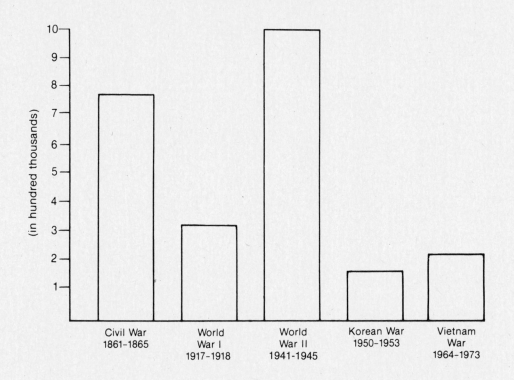

A bar graph has four parts. It has a **title**, which tells you what the graph is about. It also has a **scale** to measure amounts. The scale is usually in the left column. The graph has **labels** that tell what the bars represent. The labels are usually in the bottom row. And the graph has **bars**. Each bar stands for an amount. The longer the bar, the greater the amount.

To use a bar graph, choose the bar you are interested in. Look up to the top of the bar. Now move your eyes straight left until you cross the scale. That point on the scale tells the amount that the bar stands for.

How many American casualties were there in the Civil War? Find the bar labeled "Civil War." Look at the top of it. Then look straight left to the scale. The graph shows that there were almost 800,000 American casualties in the war.

You can also quickly compare different bars to find information. Which war caused the fewest American casualties? That is the same as asking which war is represented by the shortest bar. You can tell at a glance that the Korean War had the fewest casualties. Which is the longest bar in the graph? How many casualties does it stand for? The longest bar is labeled "World War II 1941–1945." It stands for ten hundred thousand, or a million casualties.

Try It: Reading Bar Graphs

In this bar graph, the bars go from left to right, not up and down; and the number scale is at the bottom, not at the side. Use it to answer the questions.

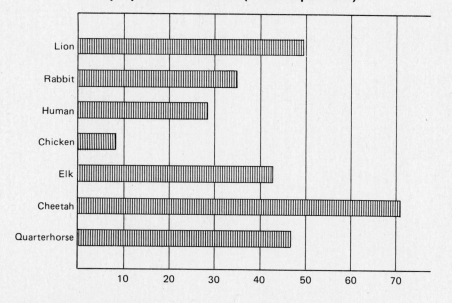

Top Speeds of Animals (in miles per hour)

1. According the bar graph, which animal is fastest?

   (1) a quarterhorse
   (2) a human
   (3) a cheetah

2. What is the top speed of a quarterhorse?

   (1) almost 60 miles an hour
   (2) almost 50 miles an hour
   (3) 29 miles an hour

3. How many miles per hour is a rabbit faster than a human?

   (1) about 5 mph
   (2) about 15 mph
   (3) about 35 mph

4. Can an elk escape a lion that is chasing it?

   (1) No, the lion is faster than the elk.
   (2) Yes, the elk is faster than the lion.
   (3) Perhaps; they both run at the same speed.

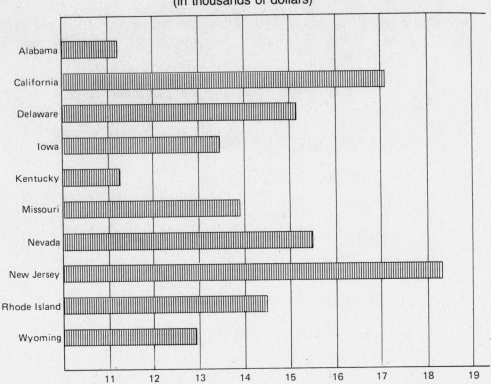

Average Income per Person in Selected States (1986)
(in thousands of dollars)

5. The average income of a person living in Missouri in 1986 was

    (1)   about $15,000
    (2)   about $14,000
    (3)   about $11,500

6. An average person in Alabama had an income similar to that of
    an average person in

    (1)   Kentucky
    (2)   New Jersey
    (3)   Wyoming

7. On average, a person who moved from Delaware to Nevada might
    earn

    (1)   a lot more money
    (2)   much less money
    (3)   about the same amount of money

Number of Calories Burned per Hour of Exercise

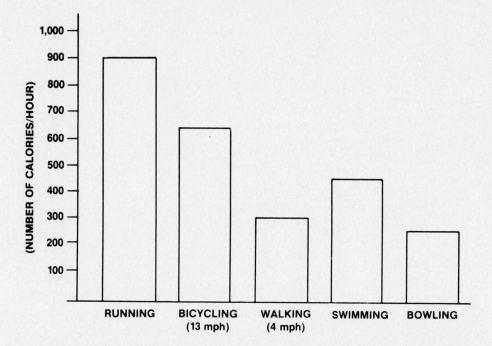

8. For which exercise do you burn the most calories in one hour?

   (1) running
   (2) bicycling
   (3) swimming

9. About how many calories would you burn if you walked for one hour?

   (1) 250   (2) 300   (3) 450

10. About how many calories would you burn if you bowled for two hours?

    (1) 250   (2) 900   (3) 500

11. Person A: ran one hour
    Person B: bicycled two hours
    Person C: walked two hours

    According to the graph, which person burned the most calories?

    (1) Person A
    (2) Person B
    (3) Person C

Check your answers on page 201.

Line Graphs

Some graphs have lines that show facts. They are called line graphs. Line graphs are very useful for showing trends—long-term patterns.

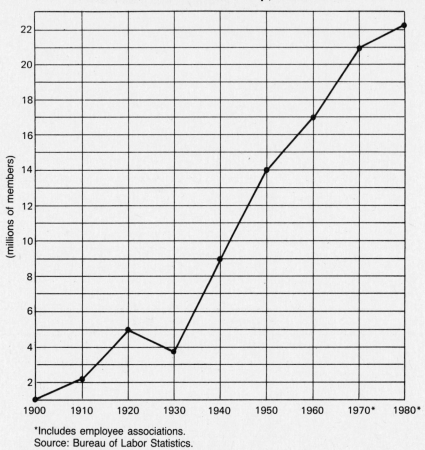

U.S. Labor Union Membership, 1900–1980

*Includes employee associations.
Source: Bureau of Labor Statistics.

A line graph has five parts. The **title** tells what the chart is about. **Labels** along the bottom usually show time; other labels along the left or right column show amounts. The **line** shows how the amounts change over time. The **footnote** gives additional information.

Look at the graph above. The line on the graph shows the number of union members from 1900 to 1980. How many union members were there in 1940? To answer the question, find 1940 in the bottom row. Go straight up until you touch the line. Then move right until you cross the number line. The answer is the number at that point on the line. You will find that there were 9 million union members in 1940.

How many union members were there in 1930? Use the same procedure to find out. You will see that there were about 4 million members in 1930. How many new members did unions gain between 1930 and 1940? Subtract 4 million from 9 million to find out: Unions gained 5 million members.

The line graph also shows trends—patterns over a period of time. What was the trend in union membership between 1920 and 1930? As you can see, the line goes down between those two dates. This means that union membership fell. What was the trend in union membership between 1930 and 1950? The line rises steeply. So did union membership, increasing from less than 4 million members to 14 million. What has happened to union membership since 1950? You can tell by the line that union membership has continued to grow, but at a slightly slower rate.

Try It: Reading Line Graphs

Look at the line graph below and answer the questions.

President's Popularity

Note: Data based on a national poll of voters.

1. What does this graph tell you?

   (1) The number of votes the president got.
   (2) The percent of people in the country who liked the president.
   (3) The percent of people who voted for the president.

2. In which year was the president most popular?

   (1) 1st year
   (2) 2nd year
   (3) 3rd year

3. According to the graph, what was the trend in the president's popularity?

(1) The president's popularity stayed the same over four years.
(2) The president's popularity went steadily down over four years.
(3) The president was more popular in the fourth year than the third year.

Announced Nuclear Weapons Tests by the US and USSR, 1945–1979

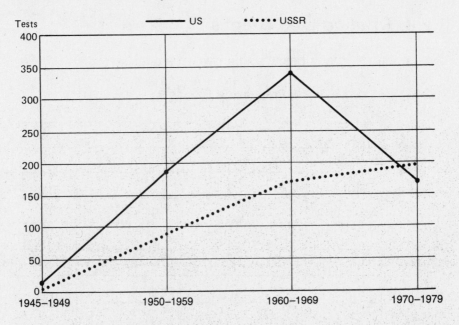

4. How many nuclear weapons tests did the United States conduct between 1950 and 1959?

(1) 89   (2) 188   (3) 344

5. How many tests did the USSR conduct between 1970 and 1979?

(1) 89   (2) 162   (3) 198

6. Weapons testing in the United States

(1) has increased each decade
(2) has always been greater than in the USSR
(3) was greatest in the years 1960–1969

Check your answers on page 202.

READING DIAGRAMS

A diagram is a picture. It shows the different parts of a thing or process. It shows how the parts work together or how a process works.

How Lenses Bend Light

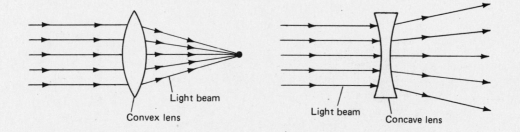

This diagram has three parts. The **title** tells you what the picture is about. The **labels** name the different parts of the diagram. The **picture** illustrates an object or process.

What is the diagram about? The title says that it is about lenses. Lenses are pieces of glass that bend light. Look carefully at the picture and the labels. Notice the shape of the lenses. The surfaces of the convex lens bend out, and the surfaces of the concave lens bend in. The arrows show the path that light takes when it passes through two different kinds of lenses. Study the paths and then answer these questions.

Which kind of lens brings light together at a point? The picture of the convex lens shows the rays of light coming together at a point. So the answer is "convex lens."

Suppose you wanted to cut down on the glare of a strong light. Which kind of lens would you use? The diagram shows light spreading out from the concave lens. That would be the lens to use to cut down glare.

Suppose you wanted to burn a hole in paper using the heat of the sun. Which kind of lens would you use? To burn a hole in paper, you need to bring the sun's light and heat onto a small spot on the paper. You would use the convex lens.

Try It: Reading Diagrams

Look at the diagram of reflecting mirrors. It shows what happens to light when it bounces off a convex and a concave mirror. Then answer the questions.

How Mirrors Bend Light

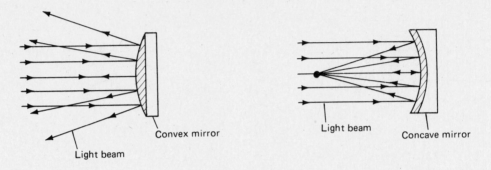

1. Which kind of mirror brings light together at a point?

    (1) concave   (2) convex

2. Which kind of mirror spreads light out?

    (1) concave   (2) convex

3. If you were building a telescope to catch the faint light from distant stars, which kind of mirror would you use?

    (1) concave   (2) convex

Check your answers on page 202.

READING MAPS

A map is another kind of diagram. It is a picture of a land area. It gives information about a region.

The Smith Lake Area

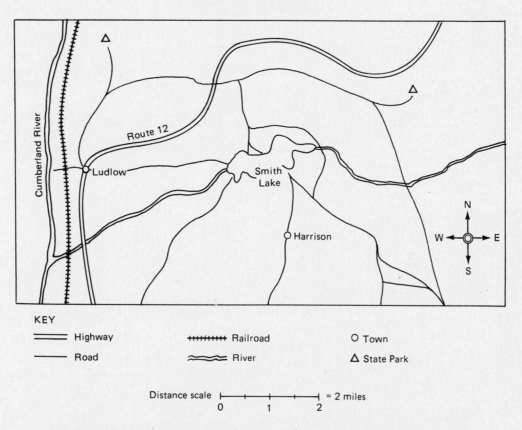

KEY

═══ Highway	┼┼┼┼┼ Railroad	○ Town
─── Road	∿∿∿ River	△ State Park

Distance scale ├───┼───┼───┤ = 2 miles
0   1   2

Maps have several parts. The **title** tells what the map shows. The **compass rose** (at the bottom) shows the directions north, south, east, and west. The **key** tells what map symbols stand for. It also has a **distance scale** that lets you measure distances. The map itself has **labels** that name places.

Study the different parts of the map. Look at the symbols in the key and find them on the map. Then answer this question: What direction would you go to travel from Harrison to Smith Lake? Draw an imaginary line between Harrison and Smith Lake on the map. Then look at the compass rose. What direction is the line you've drawn? It goes north. You would travel north to go from Harrison to Smith Lake.

Does the railroad go to Harrison? Find the symbol for railroad in the key. It is a line with little lines through it. Then find the railroad on the map. Does the railroad go to Harrison? No, it does not.

How large is Smith Lake? Take out a ruler and measure the lake. Then measure the same length on the distance scale in the key. According to the scale, how long is the lake? It is 2 miles long.

There are two main types of maps. One is the kind you just looked at. That type of map shows only a land area. Other maps contain information about a land area. These maps are often called picture maps. They can give information about a region's economy, history, natural resources, and more. Usually, you can use the same methods to read all picture maps.

World Population Density

NUMBER OF PEOPLE (DENSITY) PER SQUARE MILE

OVER 100   3–100   UNDER 3

A picture map shows a **picture** of a land area. Under the picture is a **key**. The key explains what the symbols on the map stand for. In the map above, the key is made up of boxes with labels. Each box has a different shading. Each shading stands for a different number of people per square mile.

The number of people per square mile (the "population density") is different in different parts of the world. The map shows the different densities. The darker the shading, the more people there are in a square mile. You can use the map to figure out which places have the most people and which are hardly populated at all.

Suppose you wanted to figure out the number of people per square mile in Africa. Begin by finding Africa, in the center of the map. Notice that the continent of Africa is colored in with light dots. Look at the key. The key shows that the light dots represent 3 to 100 people per square mile. This means that between 3 and 100 people live in each square mile of Africa.

Suppose you wanted to compare the populations of Africa and Europe. Which one is more densely populated? What color is Europe on the map? It is black. Look down at the key. What does black represent? It represents "over 100 people per square mile." Which part of the world is more densely populated, Africa or Europe? According to the map, Europe is more densely populated.

Try It: Reading Maps

Look at all the parts of the map. Then answer the questions.

The Tyler Region

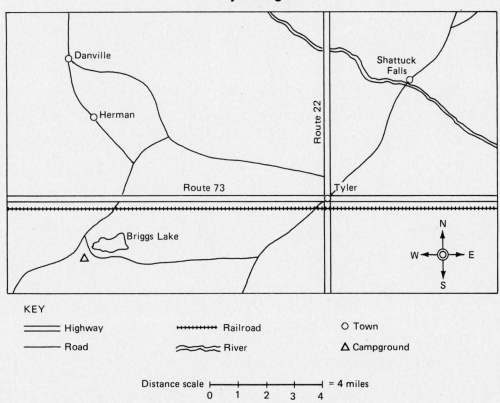

KEY

═══════ Highway ＋＋＋＋＋＋＋＋ Railroad ○ Town

─────── Road 〜〜〜〜 River △ Campground

Distance scale |———|———|———|———| = 4 miles
　　　　　　　　0　1　2　3　4

1. In what direction must you travel to go from Danville to Herman?

    (1) east　　(2) north　　(3) south

2. The railroad runs

    (1) from Tyler to Danville
    (2) alongside Route 73
    (3) to Tyler, then south

3. The campground is

    (1) about 5 miles south of Herman
    (2) about 2 miles from Tyler
    (3) just north of Briggs Lake

4. You can infer that the largest town on the map is

    (1) Danville
    (2) Tyler
    (3) Shattuck Falls

Population per Square Mile by State

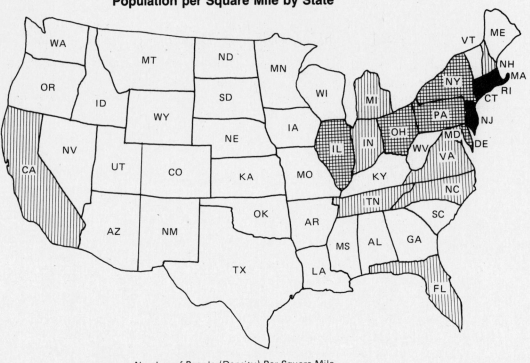

Number of People (Density) Per Square Mile

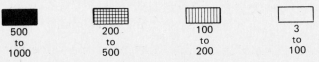

| 500 to 1000 | 200 to 500 | 100 to 200 | 3 to 100 |

5. The number of people per square mile in California (CA) is

   (1) 500 to 1000 (2) 200 to 500 (3) 100 to 200

6. The number of people per square mile in Texas (TX) is

   (1) greater than the number in Florida (FL)
   (2) more than 200
   (3) the same as the number in Louisiana (LA)

7. The states in northeastern United States

   (1) have very high population density
   (2) have very low populations
   (3) are populated about as densely as the middle parts of the country

8. From the map, you can conclude that

   (1) the population density goes down as you move from the center of the country to the east
   (2) the east coast has many large cities
   (3) the population per square mile goes down as you go from south to north

Check your answers on page 203.

UNIT REVIEW

In this unit, you've worked on reading tables, graphs, diagrams, and maps. You've seen that tables, graphs, diagrams, and maps are pictures. They are pictures that can make information easier to read and understand. You've seen how they are organized. You've seen how they help you understand information, compare facts, and see trends.

ANSWERS AND EXPLANATIONS

Try It: Reading Tables

1. **(2)** Look at the heading for Kentucky. Go across that line until you come to the column marked "Members of the House." The number there is 7.

2. **(1)** Look at the heading for New York. Then go across that line until you come to the column marked "Population." The number there is 17,557,288.

3. **(2)** Look under the heading for population. Idaho is the only state with a population under 1 million.

4. **(1)** All the states in this table have the same number of senators. But the numbers of members of the House and the populations vary.

5. **(3)** Look at the column for population. Compare this column with the column for members of the House. The states with larger populations have more members of the House.

6. **(3)** Find the heading for men (adult). Go across that line to the column marked "Vitamin C." The number there is 60.

7. **(1)** Find the heading for girls, 11–14 years. A 12-year-old girl would fall in this category. Go across that line to the column marked "Iron." The number there is 18.

8. **(2)** Find the column marked "Calcium." Go down the column to the line for girls, 11–14. The number there is 1200. Scan the calcium column. The line for boys, 11–14, has the same number.

9. **(3)** Look at the column for Vitamin B6. Scan the column. The greatest number there is 2.2. Go across the line for 2.2. You find the heading "Men (adult)."

10. **(2)** Find the heading for Houston. Go across that line to the column marked "1970." The number there is 1,233,535.

11. **(3)** Scan the column for 1980. The lowest number there is 347,862. Go across the line for that entry. You find the heading "Miami."

12. **(1)** Find the heading for Chicago. Go across that line to the column marked "1980." The number there is 3,049,479.

13. **(3)** Scan the table. The populations of some cities increased from 1970 to 1980, so (1) is wrong. Check the populations of cities in the northern U.S. (Boston, Chicago, Detroit, New York, and Philadelphia). The populations decreased, so (2) is wrong. Check the populations of cities in the Sunbelt (Houston, Miami, Phoenix). The populations have increased.

Try It: Reading Picture Graphs

1. **(1)** Find the label "1979" at the left. Count the number of $ symbols. There are 8. Multiply 8 times 100 billion.

2. **(3)** You can answer this question by eliminating the wrong choices. Answers (1) and (2) are wrong because there are more $ symbols next to 1982 than next to 1976.

3. **(2)** No row of $ symbols is shorter than the rows above it. Therefore, the debt does not go down at all. Answers (1) and (3) are therefore incorrect.

4. **(3)** Every row of $ symbols is longer than the one before it. Therefore, the trend is for the debt to increase.

Try It: Reading Circle Graphs

1. **(2)** Find the piece of the circle graph labeled "Foods, Beverages." That piece represents food and beverage exports worth $30 billion.

2. **(2)** Find the piece of the circle graph labeled "Machinery." It says that machinery made up 38.6% of U.S. exports.

3. **(1)** Find the piece of the circle graph labeled "Foods, Beverages." Look for another piece that is the same size. "Raw Materials" is about the same size. A quick check shows the values are about the same.

4. **(2)** Look at the circle graph. The largest sections are for machinery and other manufactured goods. Think about what kind of economy exports those goods. You can infer that the United States is mainly a manufacturing or industrial economy.

5. **(1)** Find the piece of the circle graph labeled "Less than 4 years of high school." It says that 21% of 18–24-year-olds did not get a high school degree.

6. **(2)** Find the piece of the circle graph labeled "4 years of high school." You can easily see that this piece makes up almost half of the circle graph. Check the label to confirm the percentage.

7. **(3)** Compare the pieces labeled "4 or more years of college" and "Less than four years of high school." The piece for high school dropouts is about three times the size of that for college graduates, so (1) is wrong. Check the number of high school dropouts to confirm that (2) is wrong.

8. **(1)** Find the pieces of the circle graph labeled "4 years of high school," "1 to 3 years of college," and "4 or more years of college." You can easily see that these pieces make up most of the circle graph—about 80%.

Try It: Reading Bar Graphs

1. **(3)** Find the longest bar on the graph. It represents the fastest animal. Read off the label for that bar.

2. **(2)** Find "Quarterhorse" in the left column. Go to the end of the bar. Then go straight down to the scale to read the answer.

3. **(1)** Compare the bars labeled "Rabbit" and "Human." The "Rabbit" bar is only a little longer than that for "Human." Check the scale. A rabbit can be only about 5 mph faster.

4. **(1)** Compare the bars labeled "Lion" and "Elk." The bar for the lion is longer.

5. **(2)** Find Missouri in the left column. Go to the end of the bar. Look straight down to the number scale and read the answer.

6. **(1)** Look at the bar labeled "Alabama." Compare its length to the bars for Wyoming, Kentucky, and New Jersey. The bar for Kentucky is the same length as the bar for Alabama.

7. **(3)** Compare the bars for Delaware and Nevada. They are both a little over $15,000.

8. **(1)** Scan the graph to see which is the longest bar. Then look down at the label for that bar for the answer.

9. **(2)** Find the bar labeled "Walking." Go to the end of the bar. Look straight left to the number scale and read the answer.

10. **(3)** Find the bar labeled "Bowling." Go to the end of the bar. Look straight left to the number scale and read off the number: 250. Now check the scale or the title of the graph. The graph shows calories burned per hour of exercise. For two hours of exercise, double the answer.

11. (2) Find the bar for each of "Running," "Bicycling," and "Walking." Then check the scale. Double the numbers for bicycling and walking to get the answers for two hours of exercise. Person A used 900 calories. Person B used about 1200 calories. Person C used 600 calories.

Try It: Reading Line Graphs

1. (2) The heading tells that the graph is about "President's Popularity." The graph is measured in percents.

2. (1) Look at the graph. The highest percent is for the first year.

3. (2) The graph declines steadily from the first through the fourth year. This means that the president's popularity went steadily down over four years.

4. (2) Find the label "1950–1959" in the bottom row. Go straight up to the "US" line—the solid line. Then go left to the number line.

5. (3) Find the label "1970–1979" in the bottom row. Go up to the dotted line that shows the USSR. Then go left to the number scale.

6. (3) (1) is wrong because U.S. tests went down between 1960 and 1980. (2) is wrong because the USSR held more tests than the U.S. in the 1970–1979 period. Between 1960 and 1969, the U.S. had 344 tests and the USSR had 162 tests.

Try It: Reading Diagrams

1. (1) Look at the path light takes in both pictures. The concave mirror shows light being bent to a point.

2. (2) Look at the path light takes in both pictures. The convex mirror shows light spreading outward.

3. (1) The more light you catch with the telescope mirror, the brighter the stars will look. You would use a mirror that brings light together—a concave mirror.

Try It: Reading Maps

1. (3) Draw an imaginary line from Danville to Herman. Use the compass rose to check the direction of the line.

2. (2) Find the symbol for "railroad" in the key. Locate the railroad on the map. It does not go from Tyler to Danville. It goes east and west, not south, from Tyler.

3. (1) Find the symbol for "campground" and locate it on the map. Use the distance scale to find that the campground is more than 2 miles from Tyler. Use the compass rose to find that the campground is west, not north, of Briggs Lake.

4. (2) Large towns grow up where important transportation routes meet. Two large roads and the railroad meet in Tyler. This is not true of Danville or Shattuck Falls. Tyler is the largest town on the map.

5. (3) Look at the shading for the state of California. Find the box in the key that has the same shading. The label gives the answer.

6. (3) Look at the shading for Texas and compare it with the shading for Florida and Louisiana. Louisiana has the same shading, and so the same population density.

7. (1) Locate the northeastern part of the country. The shading is solid black. The key tells you that shading means the population density is very high.

8. (2) (1) is wrong because population density grows as you move east. (3) is wrong because population density does not go down as you move north. The east coast has the highest number of people per square mile.

HOW MUCH CAN YOU DO NOW?

The following test will help you to see how much this book has helped you to improve your reading skills. It will also help you to see which reading skills you still need to review.

There are 40 questions in the test. Try to do all of the questions. After you finish the test, check your answers on page 218. Then fill in the chart on page 219.

Read each passage. Then choose the correct answer to the questions that follow the passage.

The cigarette industry constantly tells us that it's possible to make a safe cigarette. In the meantime, they say, cigarettes are getting safer. Is it true? Will people someday be able to puff away without fear of heart disease and lung cancer?

Not likely, according to the American Cancer Society. They say that smokers of filter cigarettes may be a little safer from lung cancer than people who smoke non-filter cigarettes. But they say that the risk of heart disease is the same for both groups. A recent study of 3,700 smokers supported this conclusion.

The results of the study started the researchers wondering. If better filters and low-tar tobacco lowered the risk of getting cancer, why was the risk of heart disease still the same? Cigarette smoke contains over 4,000 different substances, including nicotine and ammonia. Which substance was the guilty party, slipping through all those filters unchanged?

The answer was carbon monoxide, the same gas that streams out of the tailpipes of cars. Subjects from the study were tested for amounts of carbon monoxide in their blood. All showed the same high levels of carbon monoxide, whether they smoked filter or non-filter cigarettes.

Carbon monoxide is a poison. There is no way to make a cigarette that doesn't produce the gas. Carbon monoxide is formed when the tobacco burns. And no matter what the tobacco companies do to the filter, it's unlikely they can come up with a cigarette that doesn't have to be lit.

1. According to the passage, the substance in cigarette smoke that increases the risk of heart disease is

   (1) tar
   (2) nicotine
   (3) carbon monoxide
   (4) ammonia

2. From the information in the passage, you can infer that the author believes that a truly safe cigarette can never be made because

   (1) the tobacco companies don't want to spend the money for research
   (2) a burning cigarette will always produce carbon monoxide
   (3) people will always smoke non-filter cigarettes
   (4) there are over 4,000 different substances in cigarette smoke

3. With which of the following statements would the author of the passage most likely agree?

   (1) Research by tobacco companies has greatly reduced the risk of lung cancer today.
   (2) It's just a matter of time before cigarettes are completely safe.
   (3) The American Cancer Society is biased against smokers.
   (4) The cigarette industry is trying to fool the public with claims of a possibly safe cigarette.

What makes us human? How do we become individuals? How do we learn to live with other human beings?

The process of learning to live in society is called socialization. Socialization begins when a person is born. It lasts as long as the person lives.

In the early 1940's, a six-year-old girl was studied by sociologists. Her name was Isabel, and she couldn't speak. The only sounds she could make were animal-like noises. But there wasn't anything physically wrong with Isabel. She was a completely normal little girl. But Isabel had been raised alone by her mother, and her mother could not hear or speak. Isabel's mother kept her isolated in a room. She kept Isabel alone, away from people. Isabel had never heard anyone talk. She never learned to talk herself.

4. The passage implies that Isabel could not speak because she

    (1) could not hear
    (2) had a physical handicap
    (3) was emotionally disturbed
    (4) had never heard anyone speak

5. According to the passage, socialization is the process in which people

    (1) learn about their families
    (2) overcome physical handicaps
    (3) learn to live in society
    (4) gain the power of speech

6. Based on the information in the passage, which of the following statements about Isabel can be concluded?

    (1) Isabel never learned to speak because she didn't like people.
    (2) Isabel could have learned how to speak if she had heard other people speak.
    (3) Isabel could never have learned to speak because her mother could not speak.
    (4) Isabel knew how to speak, but she chose not to because she wanted to be like her mother.

Killing Germs with Heat

Germ		Temperature That Kills Germ	Time Needed to Kill Germ
Measles virus		131°F	15 minutes
Rabies virus		140°F	5 minutes
Tomato plant virus		room temp.	2 hours
Diphtheria bacteria (in water)		212°F	1 minute
TB bacteria (in milk)		212°F	10 seconds
Strep bacteria (in cream)	or	135°F 142°F	5 minutes 1 minute
Food poisoning bacteria (in can of corn)	or	212°F 239°F	105 minutes 15 minutes

7. Which germ listed in the table is killed at the lowest temperature?

    (1) measles virus
    (2) rabies virus
    (3) tomato plant virus
    (4) diphtheria bacteria

8. If you bought a can of corn and wanted to be sure you would not get food poisoning, what might you do?

    (1) Keep the corn at room temperature for 2 hours.
    (2) Heat the corn for 10 seconds at 212° F.
    (3) Heat the corn for 15 minutes at 212° F.
    (4) Heat the corn for 15 minutes at 239° F.

9. All of the following information is given in the table EXCEPT

    (1) what temperature is needed to kill a rabies virus
    (2) how long it takes to kill TB bacteria at 212° F.
    (3) how long it takes to kill strep bacteria at 212° F.
    (4) where some diphtheria bacteria can be found

In the 1850's in France, wine producers had a problem. Their sweet wine was turning sour. For centuries, winemakers knew that when grape juice sat in covered kegs, the juice turned into wine. They had never understood why the juice became alcoholic. They only knew that usually sweet, not sour, wine resulted.

The wine producers asked Louis Pasteur to help them. Pasteur was a biochemist, a scientist who studies living things. Pasteur had worked on fermentation. Fermentation is the process in which food sugars become alcohol. Pasteur knew from experiments that juice fermented with the help of microorganisms. People couldn't see these helpful microorganisms, but they changed food sugars to alcohol. Pasteur believed that some unwanted microorganisms were in the wine and were souring it.

After many experiments, Pasteur found a method of killing the unwanted germs. He heated the wine to a high temperature—about 135 degrees Fahrenheit—and then quickly cooled it. Then he poured the wine into air-tight containers. The containers were sealed to keep more unwanted microorganisms out.

Today, the method of pasteurization still keeps wine pure. It is also used to keep milk from spoiling. Campers, too, have learned a lesson from Pasteur. When they want to sterilize drinking water, they boil it.

10. Which of the following would make the best title for this passage?

    (1) The Life of Louis Pasteur
    (2) The History of Wine Making in France
    (3) The Development of the Process of Pasteurization
    (4) Pasteurization—A New Way to Make Wine

11. The word *sterilize* (last line) most nearly means

    (1) heat
    (2) purify
    (3) ferment
    (4) experiment

12. From the information in the passage, which of the following is NOT necessary for pasteurizing a liquid?

    (1) heating the liquid to 135 degrees Fahrenheit
    (2) quickly cooling the liquid after heating it
    (3) placing the liquid in an air-tight container
    (4) freezing the liquid after boiling it

4,500 years ago, some people carved great blocks of stone. They wound ropes around the blocks and, with teams of oxen, dragged them for 100 miles. When they reached a wide, open plain, they set the stones upright in a circle. Why did the people do this?

Stonehenge is a mystery. Scientists have different theories about it. Some scientists thought the monument was the work of Druids, an ancient religious people. The scientists thought that Druids may have used the stones for a temple. However, recent tests show that the stones are older than records of the Druids. Druids may have used Stonehenge, but they didn't build it. Some scientists point to bones found near the stones. They say Stonehenge may have been a tomb. Many scientists think that Stonehenge was used as a calendar. Ancient people may have measured the seasons by watching the movement of the sun between the stones. People may have decided when to plant or harvest crops by the position of the sun.

Stonehenge, located on Salisbury Plain in England, is a big tourist attraction. The English have been accused of making publicity photos that make Stonehenge look larger than it is. In fact, the stones are only a little over 12 feet high. But their mystery is still immense.

13. Which of the following best expresses the main idea of the passage?

    (1) Stonehenge is not as big as some people think it is.
    (2) Scientists still don't know who built Stonehenge or why they built it.
    (3) Stonehenge was built in a wide, open plain.
    (4) Some scientists think that Stonehenge may have been used as an ancient calendar.

14. The main purpose of the passage is to

    (1) convince you that Stonehenge was built by the Druids
    (2) provide information about the mysteries of Stonehenge
    (3) accuse the English of making Stonehenge seem larger than it really is
    (4) explain how scientists have solved the mysteries of Stonehenge

15. Based on the passage, which of the following statements does NOT describe Stonehenge?

    (1) Stonehenge is made of blocks of stone.
    (2) Stonehenge was built by the Druids.
    (3) Stonehenge is located in England.
    (4) Stonehenge is a big tourist attraction.

No nation has leaped into the 20th century like Japan. For two hundred years, Japan remained closed and isolated from the rest of the world. It was suspicious of western ways. In 1854, Commodore Perry of the U.S. Navy sailed into Tokyo Bay. When he showed the people inventions like the telegraph and railroad train, Japan realized what it was missing. Japan has quickly caught up with western technology. It may have even surpassed it.

Japan has a population of over 116,000,000. The people are thickly settled on the four main islands. Since only one sixth of the land is arable, Japan relies on imported food. To pay for the imports, Japan exports manufactured goods.

Japan builds and sells cars, motorcycles, television sets, radios, and cameras. Textiles and chemicals are also made. In Yokohama Harbor, ships are constructed for use by other nations.

The "head start" western nations had may be the reason for Japan's success today. Western countries are still using machines and technology that they developed many years ago. Japan is using newer, improved methods. For example, robots are relieving factory-line workers of long, tiring jobs.

Modern technology has brought modern problems. Air and water quality reached dangerous levels in some parts of Japan in the late 1960's. Since then, the Japanese government has applied stronger pollution controls.

16. The main idea of the passage is that Japan is

   (1)   suspicious of western ways
   (2)   an importer of food
   (3)   a technological leader today
   (4)   dealing with air and water pollution

17. With which of the following statements would the author probably NOT agree?

   (1)   Japan may have surpassed western technology.
   (2)   Robots relieve factory workers of boring jobs.
   (3)   The technological "head start" western nations had is not helping them succeed today.
   (4)   Factory workers are unhappy to be replaced by robots.

18. The word *arable* (line 11) most nearly means

   (1)   thickly settled
   (2)   farmable
   (3)   suitable for industry
   (4)   unable to be improved

Ann Hogan can't guarantee that her book will work for you, but it's worked for her. "I'm getting married next week," she says.

Ann Hogan is the 32-year-old author of *Doubles for Singles*, a guide for single men and women. She tells single people how to look, what to say, and where to find what they're looking for.

What to wear? "Always look your best," says Hogan. "Even when you go to the laundromat. Don't wear dirty T-shirts or old running shoes. You should dress as if you're going to accept an award."

What should people say to each other? "Always start with a compliment. Find something nice to say about the person you're interested in. This may take some time, so while you're waiting, smile. Smile a *lot*. If the guy or gal says something clever, or something you'd like them to *think* you think is clever, laugh."

And where should people meet? Hogan doesn't recommend bars. "It's too dark in there—you don't know what you're getting." But she thinks health clubs are good if you're not too flabby.

And how did Hogan meet her future husband? "My mother introduced us," she says.

19. From the information in the passage, you can infer that the main purpose of Ann Hogan's book *Doubles for Singles* is to help single men and women to

    (1) find better jobs
    (2) find a mate
    (3) keep up with the latest styles
    (4) get into good physical shape

20. All of the following statements about Ann Hogan are implied or stated in the passage EXCEPT

    (1) Ann Hogan is rich.
    (2) Ann Hogan is an author.
    (3) Ann Hogan is 32 years old.
    (4) Ann Hogan is getting married.

21. From the information in the passage, you can infer that Ann Hogan feels that old running shoes are

    (1) sexy
    (2) important
    (3) a sign of character
    (4) unattractive

Gross National Product of the United States, 1926–1940

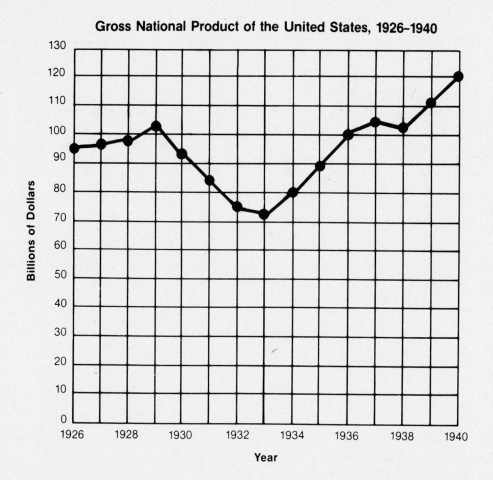

22. According to the graph, what was the gross national product of the United States in 1936?

    (1) $110 billion   (2) $100 billion
    (3) $90 billion   (4) $80 billion

23. According to the graph, in what year was the gross national product of the United States $120 billion?

    (1) 1934   (2) 1936   (3) 1938   (4) 1940

24. In which of the following years shown on the graph was the gross national product the lowest?

    (1) 1930   (2) 1932   (3) 1934   (4) 1936

25. Based on the graph, which of the following BEST describes the trend of the gross national product between 1926 and 1940?

    (1) The gross national product rose, fell, and rose again.
    (2) The gross national product remained unchanged.
    (3) The gross national product rose steadily.
    (4) The gross national product fell steadily.

Take the law. A body would think—if he wasn't very smart—that a man of law was a good man. It ain't so. Ninety per cent of the time it ain't so. A body says then, if the law ain't good, who is? Nobody.

Sheriff Claine is a good example. He used to be always poking around my store, making hints. Standing outside the front window part of the time. One evening late I got in my car and followed Sheriff Claine down the highway towards Glory Church, and then he stopped. I stopped a good piece behind him and followed him through a pine thicket to a liquor still. A whole big wildcat setup. Sheriff Claine was the ringleader of the bunch.

Next time he come to my store, I said, Sheriff, finding much wildcat whisky? He grunted and pulled up his belt and let on like business was slow. Somebody said, and I eased it to him, they's a big still down towards Glory Church, off in a pine thicket.

Sheriff Claine couldn't talk for a minute and squinted his eyes. I'll have a look, he said.

The police is just like him. They hide out at night and sleep when they're suppose to be patrolling. I've caught them at it.

26. Which of the following could best be substituted for "a body" (paragraph 1)?

    (1) a boy
    (2) a corporation
    (3) a person
    (4) a group

27. In paragraph 2, the word "wildcat" is used to mean

    (1) illegal
    (2) untame
    (3) ferocious
    (4) crazy

28. Which of the following best states the narrator's view of the relationship between police officers and civilians?

    (1) Police officers are tougher than civilians.
    (2) Police officers are no more honest than civilians.
    (3) Police officers are more honest than civilians.
    (4) Police officers can be trusted to use weapons wisely but civilians cannot.

Can you believe what you read? Laurence Bickert is a free-lance journalist. He says he has a lot of respect for newspapers, but he thinks most people have too much. "They believe without questioning," he says.

One day last year, Bickert was reading a major daily newspaper. It had an article about a teacher from Bickert's hometown who had won a national award. "I read the article and turned the page. Suddenly I realized that hardly a fact in the article had been right. It had the name of the teacher's school wrong. It had the name of his teaching specialty wrong. It even had the number of children in his family wrong. This article wasn't so important. But what about issues of national interest? How many facts are we getting straight?"

Another thing Bickert advises readers to look out for is bias. "All writers are human, and it's only human to have an opinion. But sometimes opinion gets in the way of the news. When you're reading about how poor or rich a country is, think about the newspaper and the writer. Are they giving you an open-minded picture? Or is their reporting slanted?" Bickert advises people to get their news from as many different sources as possible. "That way, even when the news is biased, all the different viewpoints help you form a clearer picture for yourself."

29. Which of the following statements best describes Laurence Bickert's feelings toward newspapers?

(1) People shouldn't always believe everything that they read in a newspaper.
(2) People shouldn't read newspapers because newspapers always distort the truth.
(3) Newspaper writers are more careful about the facts than most other writers.
(4) Newspapers have a right to be less careful about stories that aren't so important.

30. From the passage, you can infer that the word *biased* (line 23) most nearly means

(1) informative
(2) complete
(3) important
(4) slanted

31. According to the passage, Laurence Bickert thinks that one of the ways people can get the facts about a story is to

(1) trust their favorite newspaper
(2) read as many different newspapers as possible
(3) watch the news on TV
(4) read a major newspaper

In the late 1860's, industry in America grew rapidly. More factories meant more jobs. But working conditions were hazardous. Employees were forced to work as many as 16 hours a day in hot, dirty rooms. Children often worked alongside adults. Wages were usually very low.

Workers tried to improve conditions by forming unions. One of the first important unions was the Knights of Labor, formed in 1869. Blacks and women were welcomed as members. The Knights of Labor wanted an 8-hour workday, higher wages, and better working conditions. The union called for an end to the employment of children under age 14.

Together with other unions, the Knights of Labor tried to make changes through collective bargaining. Union leaders would meet with employers and talk. When collective bargaining failed, the unions resorted to strikes. When some strikes that the unions held turned violent, public opinion turned against them. Many members left the Knights of Labor, and by 1890 the union died out.

But other unions survived. The AF of L, American Federation of Labor, was formed in 1881. It continued to push for the goals set by the Knights of Labor. However, most federal laws protecting workers and outlawing child labor were not passed until the 1930's.

32. According to the passage, the Knights of Labor wanted all of the following EXCEPT

   (1) an 8-hour workday
   (2) higher wages
   (3) improved working conditions
   (4) unemployment benefits

33. You can infer that most of the goals of the Knights of Labor were

   (1) unwelcomed by the AF of L
   (2) not reached until after the Knights of Labor died out
   (3) not helpful to women
   (4) welcomed by factory owners

34. Which of the following statements about labor unions can be concluded based on the information in the passage?

   (1) Labor unions reached their peak of power in the 1860's.
   (2) It took labor unions many years to improve conditions for workers.
   (3) The early labor unions failed because they were not concerned with the well-being of workers.
   (4) The early labor unions failed because they could not agree on what they wanted to fight for.

When you walk across a rug and then touch a doorknob, you may feel a "shock." This shock is the result of static electricity. What is static electricity? All electricity is caused by charged particles inside the atom. Protons have a positive electrical charge. Electrons have a negative electrical charge. When there is an equal number of each in the atom, the charges balance out. Then the atom as a whole has no electrical charge. When two objects are rubbed together, however, one of them may give up electrons to the other. Then the one that gained electrons has a negative charge. The one that lost electrons has a positive charge. The atoms of both objects have now become ions.

When you walk across a rug, your body picks up electrons from the rug. Your body becomes negatively charged. Then when you touch a doorknob, the negative ions on your hand give up their extra electrons. These electrons flow to the doorknob. That flow of electrons is the static electricity that gives you a shock.

35. Which of the following statements best gives the main idea of the passage?

   (1) You often feel a shock when you walk across a rug and then touch a doorknob.
   (2) Static electricity is not understood by scientists.
   (3) Static electricity is caused by a flow of electrons.
   (4) When you walk across a rug, your body picks up electrons from the rug.

36. From the passage, you can infer that an atom becomes electrically charged when it

   (1) gains or loses a proton
   (2) gains or loses an electron
   (3) has an equal number of protons and electrons
   (4) comes into contact with any other atom

37. According to the passage, an atom has no electrical charge when

   (1) it has an equal number of protons and electrons
   (2) it gives up its electrons to another atom
   (3) it does not contain any protons
   (4) it becomes an ion

Nick sat quiet.

"You came out of it damned well," Bill said. "Now she can marry somebody of her own sort and settle down and be happy. You can't mix oil and water and you can't mix that sort of thing any more than if I'd marry Ida that works for Strattons. She'd probably like it, too."

Nick said nothing. The liquor had all died out of him and left him alone. Bill wasn't there. He wasn't sitting in front of the fire or going fishing tomorrow with Bill and his dad or anything. He wasn't drunk. It was all gone. All he knew was that he had once had Marjorie and that he had lost her. She was gone and he had sent her away. That was all that mattered. He might never see her again. Probably he never would. It was all gone, finished.

"Let's have another drink," Nick said.

38. When the author says "Bill wasn't there," he means

   (1) Nick couldn't see Bill
   (2) Bill went away for a few minutes
   (3) Bill was angry at Nick
   (4) Bill's presence could not comfort Nick

39. Which of the following best expresses the central idea of the passage?

   (1) Nick was feeling down, but he knew he'd soon be feeling better.
   (2) Bill was successfully helping Nick to get over his pain.
   (3) Nick was trying to forget Marjorie.
   (4) Nick felt as though his world had ended because his relationship with Marjorie had ended.

40. Which of the following descriptions of the relationship between Nick and Marjorie is true?

   (1) They were married.
   (2) They had been childhood sweethearts.
   (3) Prior to their breakup, they had been inseparable.
   (4) The differences between them made their relationship difficult.

ANSWER KEY

1.	(3)	11.	(2)	21.	(4)	31.	(2)
2.	(2)	12.	(4)	22.	(2)	32.	(4)
3.	(4)	13.	(2)	23.	(4)	33.	(2)
4.	(4)	14.	(2)	24.	(2)	34.	(2)
5.	(3)	15.	(2)	25.	(1)	35.	(3)
6.	(2)	16.	(3)	26.	(3)	36.	(2)
7.	(3)	17.	(4)	27.	(1)	37.	(1)
8.	(4)	18.	(2)	28.	(2)	38.	(4)
9.	(3)	19.	(2)	29.	(1)	39.	(4)
10.	(3)	20.	(1)	30.	(4)	40.	(4)

In this chart, circle the number of any item that you did not answer correctly. The right-hand side of the chart will tell you the units to review for any item that you missed.

Item number:	Unit to study:
11 18 26 27 30	UNIT 3: Using Clues to Unlock Word Meanings
16 35	UNIT 4: Finding the Main Idea
1 5 12 15 20 31 32 37	UNIT 5: Finding Details
10 13 28 29 39	UNIT 6: Finding the Unstated Main Idea
2 4 19 21 33 36 38 40	UNIT 7: Making Basic Inferences; UNIT 8: Using Organization to Make Inferences
6 34	UNIT 9: Drawing Logical Conclusions
3 14 17	UNIT 10: Recognizing Facts and Opinions; UNIT 11: Identifying Bias and Tone
7 8 9 22 23 24 25	UNIT 12: Reading Tables, Graphs, Diagrams, and Maps

ACKNOWLEDGMENTS

Page 11: From "Haircut" by Ring Lardner. Copyright 1925, 1953 by Ellis A. Lardner. In *The Best Short Stories of Ring Lardner*, copyright 1957 by Charles Scribner's Sons. Reprinted by permission.

Pages 13 and 65: From *Working* by Studs Terkel. Copyright 1972, 1974 by Studs Terkel. Published by arrangement with Pantheon Books, a division of Random House.

Page 16: From "Fresh Fruits and Vegetables Incorporated" by Andrew A. Rooney. In *And More by Andy Rooney*. Reprinted with the permission of Atheneum Publishers.

Page 66: Adapted from *The Magnificent Adventures of Alexander Mackenzie* by Philip Vail. Published by Dodd, Mead & Co. Copyright 1964 by Philip Vail.

Page 72: Adapted from *Man of the House* by Tip O'Neill, with William Novak. Published by Random House. Copyright 1987 by Thomas P. O'Neill, Jr.

Page 83: Adapted from "The Leader of the People" by John Steinbeck. In *Studies in the Short Story*, published by Holt, Rinehart, and Winston, 1968.

Page 92: Adapted from *The Little Prince* by Antoine de Saint Exupery; translated by Katherine Woods. Published by Harbrace Paperbound Library, Harcourt, Brace & World. Copyright 1943 by Harcourt, Brace, & World.

Page 207: Table adapted from Philip L. Altman and Dorothy S. Dittmer, *Biology Data Book*. Federation of American Societies for Experimental Biology, 1964.

Page 213: From "This Is My Living Room" by Thomas McAfee. In *Poems & Stories* and *Whatever Isn't Glory*. Copyright by Thomas McAfee.

Page 217: From Ernest Hemingway, "The Three-Day Blow." In *In Our Time*, copyright 1925 by Charles Scribner's Sons; copyright renewed. Reprinted by permission.